Finish Well is a great read! As you explore the depth and richness of author Rod Ellis' extensive life experience in pastoral leadership, you'll be left with the impression that you've made a new friend. But more importantly, Ellis will give you a fresh perspective of the God who loves you and destines a bright hope for your future. Ellis' tone is warm and engaging, and his message is clear: no matter what stage of life you're in, you, too, can explore and experience a truly abundant life.

—Gary Bennett, Pastor (retired)
Victoria First Church of the Nazarene

I found this excellent book a great read and only wish that I would have had that kind of a resource at the beginning of my "race". Every Christ follower could find great benefit from reading and practicing the clear path laid out in *Finish Well*. Rod has gifted us with an excellent biblically principled and personally illustrated road map for "finishing well".

—Arnie Toews, Clinical Counsellor
Founder of Pacific Rim Counselling in Victoria, British Columbia, a Counselling Centre, and a masters degree program at Uganda Christian University.

Rod Ellis has distilled decades of experience to give us practical, actionable tips along with insightful Biblical teaching. Whatever your stage of life, Finish Well will help you focus on the key priorities of a life well lived. I am approaching retirement and so "finishing well" has a timely message for me. For all of us it sets the course for the road ahead.

—Canon Brian McVitty, Pastor
Celebration Church in Barrie, Ontario

Being in Christian leadership is not a task for the faint of heart. There are pitfalls and dangers to avoid. Rod Ellis reminds the reader of the principle of "how one starts determines one's ending", as your starting point determines your trajectory. If we begin and build on a solid biblical foundation it will follow that the entire building will last and be a testament to God's faithfulness and grace in your life and leadership. Mixing personal history, theology, and stories of God's people throughout Biblical history, Rod encourages the individual reader or small group to reflect on how they might apply what is written in order to "finish well"!

—Darin Reimer, Executive Director
Sanctuary Youth Centre in Victoria, British Columbia

As a member of Rod Ellis' former flock at Church of Our Lord, I was greatly blessed by his wise teaching and shepherding. Now again, I have been challenged and encouraged by his book, *Finish Well*. Rod seamlessly weaves scriptural examples and teaching with his own life experiences as he encourages his readers to continue diligently growing until life's earthly end in order to be conformed to the glorious image of Christ.

—Laine Warden, Church Member
Church of Our Lord

Finish Well is in a word, excellent! Whatever stage of life you're in—whether at the beginning, middle, or close to the end—this book will serve as a very good and helpful guide. It is full of wisdom and sound advice, based as it is on God's Word and on Rod Ellis' life experiences, encouragement as we deal with challenges in our personal lives and in the fast-changing world in which we live, and hope for the future in our Saviour, Jesus Christ. The questions at the end of each chapter are challenging and conducive to much lively discussion—a great book to use in a home group.

I feel very privileged to have been one of the sheep in Rod's Church of Our Lord flock from 2006 to 2017. He was such a good shepherd, a fine example of how to live as a follower of Jesus, and he displayed in abundance the fruits of the Holy Spirit."

—Diane Liang, Church Warden & Elder
Church of Our Lord

In *Finish Well*, Rod Ellis describes how to start life right by having abiding faith in the God of the Bible, how to live life abundantly by trusting in God to cause all *"all things work together for good to them that love [Him]"* (Romans 8:28, KJV) and fulfill His purpose, and how to prepare to finish well. Throughout this spiritual memoir, Rod shares lessons learned from life's hardships and spiritual insights he gained over seventy years. Many are based on the Bible-based, practical messages he preached as a pastor for forty years, and practiced in life, as he "walked the talk".

Each chapter provides questions that will cause readers to examine their own lives in order to unlearn the thinking and practices that aren't working, and relearn what will produce a more abundant life and earn a *"well done, good and faithful servant"* (Matthew 25:23, KJV) finish before entering a new beginning in heaven.

—Dr. William A. Gray
Author of *Why Become a Christian: A Spiritual Memoir* and *God Nods on True Love*
President of Mentoring Solutions

Rev. Dr. Rod Ellis is a very engaging author who draws you in through his storytelling from the Bible and his personal life. Are you wondering how to finish life well? If so, Rod has much wisdom to share with you.

A Guide to Starting Right and Living Abundantly

FINISH Well

ROD ELLIS

Printed in Canada

Soft Cover ISBN: 978-1-4866-1976-4
Hardcover ISBN: 978-1-4866-1977-1
eBook ISBN: 978-1-4866-1978-8

Word Alive Press
119 De Baets Street Winnipeg, MB R2J 3R9
www.wordalivepress.ca

Cataloguing in Publication information can be obtained from Library and Archives Canada.

I dedicate this book to my parents who set an example for my brother, sister and me of starting right with a solid foundation. I give thanks for my father, Leslie, who showed us the importance of being a close-knit family, and for my mother, Kathleen, who encouraged us to reach out and to make the most of every opportunity.

Contents

FOREWORD

Finish Well is much more than a mere look-back at Rod Ellis' decades-long career of serving God and the human beings God has placed under his care, it is an articulate work of what I would call "heroic humility". Beginning with his upbringing and somewhat riotous youth in South Africa he tells a tale of moving from one unexpected challenge to another, following his acceptance of God-in-Christ's invitation to a life of intimacy and repentance—understood as the continuing re-focus of his attention away from himself and toward God. This fruit manifested through turning a failing congregations around, accepting responsibility when he occasionally over-reached, and reaching out into the communities in which he served to lead the dynamic ministries extra-parochial ministries that changed them. These efforts were birthed in nothing but vision—from God Himself—and the courage to "declare it" until people and resources came alongside to share both the burden and the honour.

This book is a must-read for leaders and those who have a fleshly idea of what constitutes leadership—whether in the Church or in the world. It is just as crucial for anyone who thinks Jesus' direction to "count the cost before setting on a journey" means pulling back when that cost proves overwhelming to our current resources. On the contrary, it is the Lord's challenge that anything worth doing for Him is doable only in Him—He perfects his strength in our weakness, after all, not our strength.

My guess is Rod himself will be embarrassed when he reads this as he knows himself all too well as a flawed human being well aware of the old saw, "evangelism is just one beggar telling another where to find some bread". The reality is, however, that God consistently chooses people like Rod—or temperamental zealots like Paul of Tarsus and obsessive over-achievers like Martha of Bethany—to be the bearers of His utterly empowering trust.

Finish Well is full of inspiring stories of a life lived in dependence, a will to respond to surprise, and bits of wisdom found in unexpected places. Its power, however, is in the picture of a self-described unremarkable son who showed up to work at the vineyard (Matthew 21:28-32) after first saying he would not. Rod Ellis is an engaging and expressive writer and his book is an enjoyable read, but he is a better servant and a supremely inspiring example of what happens when a regular guy says, *"not my will, but yours be done"* (Luke 22:42b, NIV).

James A Wilson, President of PrayNorthState Maverick Ministries
Author of *The Holy Spirit and the End-times* and *Generation*

INTRODUCTION

Having hit the biblical three score and ten (which means I am past being a mere senior) and having finished a forty-year career, I am now officially retired. This means that remembering the past is a natural pastime. As I look back on my life, I find opposites can both be true: I see failure and success, strength and weakness, joy and sadness, peace and conflict, and much more.

It is easy to look back but it can be harder to look forward. Having led and been part of many Alpha courses, I have been deeply blessed by Nicky Gumbel's very natural way of communicating important life lessons and truths. My imagination was captured by one question in the Alpha book *Questions of Life*, "How do we make the most of the rest of our lives?"[1] This book is my effort to honour this question.

Aging is not something most of us take much interest in until we start to get old. We may watch parents having to cope with old age or start to be affected ourselves by aches and pains, beginning to discover our own limitations.

Why do some people remain so active, involved, committed, and hardworking well into their seventies, eighties, and even nineties, while others shrivel up and withdraw into sedentary retirement as they wait to die? Some of us grow old and

---

[1] Gumbel, Nicky, *Questions of Life* (Colorado Springs: Cook Communication Ministries, 1996), page 233.

mature with grace, dignity and sweetness, while others become more sour, bitter and childish. Some of us never quite get used to the idea of aging and continue in denial until our last gasp.

The key is to be prepared to make the most of whatever age we are now. This is true however young or old we think we are. The well-loved Christian evangelist Billy Graham wrote a biography, *Nearing Home,* in which he said of those who age well, "For them growing older was not something to be denied or dreaded; it was to be embraced as part of God's plan for their lives." It reminds me of the wise saying: for the best results, follow the instructions of the maker. Just as the best way to start the day is to eat a good breakfast, the best way to make the most of each day is to fuel up with a good spiritual breakfast. If we want to finish well, we begin by considering and consulting with the One who says, "*I am the Alpha and the Omega, the First and the Last, the Beginning and the End*" (Revelation 22:13). Then we discover that this and every day is the day He has made, and we can rejoice, make the most of every opportunity, and enjoy life in abundance.

We can make today either the enemy or the friend of tomorrow. It all depends on our choices and actions in this moment, choices that will affect the future. I want to finish well so it is my hope every day to reflect and regroup, reset and reboot, revive and recycle, refresh and recreate as I continue to fulfill my life's commission.

Many other people have considered this topic, some with more knowledge and more research than I have done, but my hope in writing this book is that the perspective and principles, experience and expertise of a septuagenarian and simple pastor are unique and hopefully resonant enough to be useful to others who also want to finish well.

CHAPTER 1
In the Beginning

Generally, we have no control over our birth or our death. Our start in life is determined by many factors—the family, country, culture and belief system into which we are born—while death can come as our bodies wear out or as our lifespan is shortened by illness or fatal injury.

Where we *do* have input is in what happens between birth and death. We can choose whether to be hindered by circumstances or to rise above them. We all have times where we take a step forward and other times take a step back. For some there is overall advancement while others experience a steady or sharp decline. Where we end up is determined by where we start but also where we restart over and over again through the many challenges and stages of life.

I look back and recognize in my own life many new beginnings, often preceded by endings. Beginning at a new school means moving from another school; beginning a life together in marriage involves ending singleness; beginning a new job means coping with change; beginning a family means the end of a full night sleep, for a while anyway; moving house means leaving behind memories. I can remember those life changes as though they were yesterday and will share some of them over the course of these pages. But as my retirement is still fresh, I'll start with that change.

More than two years ago, after completing forty years of ordained ministry, I entered the new stage of retirement. The first month or two was great. I enjoyed a vacation, a college reunion in England, and the enjoyment of being free from the pressures of daily ministry. With new vigor, I began to write another book and was open to ministry where I was invited. Every morning I headed to what I called my "office" in our local sports centre. I enjoyed meeting the Lord in my devotions, reading the Word, and worshipping at our local church on Sunday afternoons, often visiting churches in the mornings. I continued to be involved on mission boards and committees. Yet out of nowhere, several months in, I fell into a funk. I did not feel like attending meetings, planning, dealing with problems, or even reading a book, let alone writing one. I know I am not alone in such post-retirement blues, so what happened? I'll ask you to hold that question until we look at life stages. For now, I will say that if we want to finish well, no matter what our age, setting a solid foundation is our starting point.

A good place to start is at the beginning. That's why I want to turn to the first verse of the first chapter of Genesis, which means origin or source.

"In the beginning, God…" (Genesis 1:1a). This verse goes to the very heart and purpose of the whole Bible. It sets the course for our understanding of Scripture, God, life, truth, reality and pretty much everything. It is an introduction to the Author, and an introduction to His intent. Verse 1 is not an invitation to debate God's existence or an offering of a theory. It is simply a statement of fact, and a declaration of intent. The same is true of the opening of John's Gospel, *"In the beginning was the Word, and the Word was with God, and the Word was God"* (John 1:1). The same truth is consistent throughout the Scriptures from beginning to end. It is incredible that so many experiences of so many different people living in different stages of history are drawn together by this unified and underscored theme.

Some may ask whether we can believe the Bible in the face of new scientific discoveries. In a word, yes, absolutely, and here is why. Truth is truth, whatever the source. We can draw a distinction between discovered truth and truth revealed through the Word of God. Science observes, evaluates and comes to a conclusion or hypothesis. It attempts to answer the question, how, and perhaps, when. The word theology comes from the Greek *theos* meaning God and *logos* meaning study. The study of God answers the questions why and, even more importantly, who.

Some try to polarize science and theology. In the sixteenth century, for instance, Galileo proposed that the earth was not the centre of the universe. The church leaders of the day refused to accept his findings and set their understanding of revelation truth against scientific discovery. As believers, we need to avoid falling into the same trap. At the other extreme, some scientists conclude there is only one acceptable truth, based on their criteria of observable data, and that God cannot be part of the equation. The Apostle Paul offers an interesting comment on such people: "*Although they claimed to be wise, they became fools and exchanged the glory of the immortal God for images made to look like a mortal human being and birds and animals and reptiles*" (Romans 1:22, 23).

Many people think scientists can't possibly believe in God. While many are not believers, some scientists who've made important discoveries were and are Christian. To quote Albert Einstein, "Science without religion is lame, religion without science is blind." Sir Isaac Newton, the great scientist who discovered the laws of gravity, said, "Gravity can explain the nature of the planets, but it cannot explain who set the planets in motion." Other committed believers include Louis Pasteur who was instrumental in developing the germ theory of disease, and developing pasteurization, Gregor Mendel, a founder of genetics, Blaise Pascal who had much to do with the development of calculus and the theory of probability, and Johannes Kepler who is considered to be the founder of astronomy. Throughout history many scientists have been professing Christians. The same is true today.

WHO IS GOD?

We appreciate it when people recognize us by name, and we are protective of the honour of our name. Names are important in establishing our sense of identity. Most of us have three names—a first, middle and surname—while some have many more. We also have titles and functions associated with our names, all of which describe our identity. We should not be surprised that God has many names describing who He is.

The Hebrew word used in Genesis 1:1 is *elohim*, the all-mighty, all-powerful One. In the midst of a pantheon of gods of different cultures, God is introduced as the supreme, powerful Creator.

We have a hard time comprehending beyond the tangible and finite. We want evidence, like Thomas, the apostle who wanted to see and touch, and who said, "*Unless I see the nail marks in his hands and put my finger where the nails were, and put my hand into his side, I will not believe*" (John 20:25). It's impossible for us to comprehend a universe that is expanding at an accelerating rate, let alone to begin to comprehend God.

This is impossible for us, but God took the trouble to reveal Himself to His creation. God is outside of and not limited by time. Before anything else came into existence, God is.

When Moses has an encounter with God, he asks a valid question, "Who are you?" God introduces himself as "*I AM Who I AM*" (Exodus 3:14). This is represented in Hebrew as JHWH, from which we get another name for God, Yahweh. God, Elohim, the Lord Creator God is one and the same as Yahweh, the Pre-Existent Eternal One.

Isaiah introduces another name, *Immanuel,* meaning God with us (Isaiah 7:14). The Lord God Almighty and Eternal is not distant and unapproachable, but is with us, alongside us, in the midst of us.

In the first chapter of his Gospel, John introduces God as the Word, an expression and communication of His thought, and intent: *"The Word become flesh and made His dwelling among us. We have seen His glory..."* (John 1:14). God took human form, became incarnate in the physical realm within the limitations of space and time so that we might catch a glimpse of His heavenly kingdom, and see His glory.

We know God because God who is spirit took the initiative to reveal Himself to us in the person of Jesus. If we have seen Jesus, the Word, we have seen the Father, Elohim, Yahweh. Jesus says to a questioning Philip, *"Anyone who has seen me has seen the Father"* (John 14:9). Even more, Paul writes,

The Son is the image of the invisible God, the firstborn over all creation. For in Him all things were created: things in heaven and on earth, visible and invisible, whether thrones or powers or rulers or authorities; all things have been created through Him and for Him. He is before all things, and in Him all things hold together. (Colossians 1:15-17)

BIG BANG OR BIG GOD?

When we move farther into that first verse in Genesis, we read, *"In the beginning God created the heavens and the earth"* (Genesis 1:1). This tells us that God already existed before the existence of the world as we know it. His thought, His Word was there. Then He brought about the creation of heaven and earth, the cosmos, our known universe. But how? Doesn't the scientific explanation contradict the Bible?

It depends on our worldview. Deists believe in a Creator, but one who is impersonal and disconnected from creation. Theists believe in a Creator who sustains and is involved in His creation. Theism starts from a belief that the biblical account is not only true but does not contradict science. Naturalism is a-theistic or anti-theistic and starts from the position that natural processes offer the most rational explanation for understanding our natural world. This would include a denial of the supernatural and therefore a Creator God.

We have to decide which makes more sense: naturalism with its premise, 'In the beginning energy,' or theism which believes in the design of a creative mind and power?

Let's consider two scientific theories that naturalist atheists love to say disprove God.

The first is the Big Bang theory, that the universe came into being through an explosion some 13.7 billion years ago. To believe that a blast somewhere in space evolved into the order and intricacy of this universe takes quite a stretch of faith. It is like believing that a bomb blast in a library could create an encyclopedia. This doesn't even begin to cover human personality, soul and spirit. Is this any more tenable than considering an agent, cause, designer, creator? Even if a blast was the means used to start the process, for the end result, I believe that an intelligent designer had to be its architect.

The second theory believed to disprove God and the Bible is that of evolution. Darwin's 1859 *Origin of the Species* observed natural evolution within the species over many years. I don't have a problem with the broad sense of the word evolution where it means development, change and adaptation. However, discovered truth should complement and be confirmed by revelation truth. The Bible tells us that God created living creatures *"according to their kinds"* (Genesis 1:24).

IT WAS GOOD

So how was the world created? *"In the beginning God created the heavens and the earth. Now the earth was formless and empty, darkness was over the surface of the deep, and the Spirit of God was hovering over the waters"* (Genesis 1:1, 2).

While there are many different Christian views of Creation, I will discuss three.

- The literal six-day view says that God can do anything. If Jesus could perform miracles instantaneously, He could create the universe in six days.

- The day/age theory suggests that if a thousand years are like a day to God, God could have created the universe in a process over time.
- The gap theory espouses a gap between the first two verses of Genesis 1. God created the universe through cosmic evolution before a cataclysmic event destroyed life on earth rendering it formless and empty. He then began the process of bringing form and order, light and life to the earth as described from verse 2 onwards.

I have no problem with any of these views, although I lean toward the age theory. To me what is essential is that Christians are united in the belief that God is the intentional Source and Creator of the universe. The Bible doesn't offer technical information on how and when. As we have mentioned, the real question is why, which leads to the main question, who.

God's purpose was to bring order out of chaos, form out of formlessness. Each day described in Genesis 1 represents a new order of creation. The universe is created by Him and for Him. Just as we have a natural desire to make a home for ourselves, so God is creating a place to dwell. In Genesis 1, God takes the raw materials He created and uses them to create a place fit for habitation. The scientific theories on how this was accomplished are all interesting. But let me be bold to say, without reference to the God whose idea it was in the first place, they give us nothing! With Him, everything makes sense—in Him, all He created is good.

In this process, however long it took, God took what was empty and filled it, bringing order from chaos. He created time, weather, seasons, agriculture and living creatures, all preparing an environment to be His temple, the jewel in His universe. Everything He created was good, and by the time He had finished, *"God saw all that He had made, and it was very good"* (Genesis 1:31). On the seventh day (the number of perfection or completion), *"He rested from all His work"* (Genesis 2:2).

Was this because He was exhausted and had to put up His feet and recover? Some interpret rest instead as taking up residence. His home was ready, and He could move in, enjoy it. This did not limit His omnipresence and transcendence beyond space and time. We have all had the experience of fixing up a new place, moving in, and then resting as we enjoy our home. God was pleased with His new dwelling.

However, like any house, it needed people to make it a home. The final part of the process was in creating humankind, making people as male and female in

His own image, to enjoy fellowship with Him and to be stewards or caretakers of this home. God commissions them to fill the earth, subdue and rule over it (Genesis 1:29). He blesses them and provides everything they need to be fruitful and to enjoy His creation. *"You have made them a little lower than the angels and crowned them with glory and honor. You made them rulers over the works of your hands; you put everything under their feet"* (Psalm 8:5, 6).

Let me briefly mention two very practical applications about what it means to be stewards of God's creation: Christians should be at the forefront of preserving our environment rather than leaving it to those who don't even acknowledge their Creator. Second, we need to truly remember the Sabbath and keep it holy.

Like the stewardship responsibility, our Sabbath obligation is directly related to our belief that all beginnings are centred in Him. It remembers that on the sixth day of creation, God Himself rested. When Jesus said *"The Sabbath was made for man"* (Mark 2:27), He tells us that Sabbath rest is for our benefit. It is important to build in recreative rest into our week, but Sabbath means more. As Christians we remember the first day of the week inaugurated by the early Church to celebrate Jesus's resurrection. We come together in worship to welcome Him into His temple, to give thanks to Him for inviting us into His confidence, and to acknowledge His Lordship over all creation—the natural and the spiritual, His world and His Church. Getting this basic principle right provides us with a right start to our week, and to fulfilling God's commission in our lives.

God never just started the universe and then let it run its course. His involvement and communication with His creation began at the beginning and continues through history. He does this by His Spirit, the same one that hovered over the waters of Creation, and His spoken Word.

In the past God spoke to our ancestors through the prophets at many times and in various ways, but in these last days He has spoken to us by His Son, whom He appointed heir of all things, and through whom He made the universe. (Hebrews 1:1, 2)

Jesus demonstrated His Lordship over nature, over physical laws through miracles (such as in the stilling of the storm), over death by His resurrection, and over the spiritual world by casting out demons and restoring sanity.

From Genesis through the Old and New Testaments, we see God seeking to make His home among us in the world He created for His purpose and His pleasure.

LET THERE BE LIGHT

One of the most important and attractive qualities of a home is the lighting — whether natural light, or through electricity and light bulbs. Natural light coming in large windows is one of the features we love about our present home. God is all about light and this was the first element in His created order. "*And God said, 'Let there be light' and there was light. God saw that the light was good, and He separated the light from the darkness*" (Genesis 1:3-4).

One of the questions raised from this passage in Genesis is that of why light is mentioned before the creation of the sun and moon. This question shows the limitations of trying to interpret revelation truth with scientific methods. Where we start determines the lens with which we view the world around us, and where we end up in life decisions and issues. In Scripture, light is more than just the light given by the sun or electricity. It has a variety of meanings: from the character and values of God, to revelation and unveiling of the truth, to the very presence and glory of God shining in all His brilliance. Jesus is described as the light of the world: "*In Him was life, and that life was the light of all mankind. The light shines in the darkness, and the darkness has not overcome it*" (John 1:4, 5). The Christian life is not dull, dreary and miserable. The closer to the light of Christ we get, the more we see His Life. Jesus gives life full of colour, brightness and fullness.

As a long-time tennis lover, I have the greatest respect for one of the greatest players ever, Roger Federer. If Roger offered to spend time to play with me, to coach, support, and encourage my game, what a privilege that would be. As a student of life, it is an even higher privilege to have the Creator, Lord and God of the universe offering to come alongside me and give me His love, support and direction. Instead of living in black and white, I enjoy life in full high-definition colour!

Contrast this with an atheistic view. What is the hope, the good news, the life offered by atheism, or for that matter naturalism, paganism or secular humanism? What is life separated from the One who is life and light? When we think we don't need God, that we can do it "my way," by making our own rules and deciding for ourselves what is good or evil, we are simply putting ourselves in God's place.

Looking around at a world that has turned its back on God we see disorder and chaos, misery and emptiness, death and destruction. Without true life and light, existence is reduced to meaningless effort with nothing to look forward to but oblivion. To borrow from the myth of Sisyphus, it is like continually rolling a stone up a hill only to have it roll all the way back again, and then doing the same again and again *ad infinitum*. When we do away with revealed truth and focus only on discovered truth, we reduce truth to only what we understand. That is extremely small in relation to the infinite, eternal, expansive nature of God. It comes down to the basis for life. When we start with God, it radically changes our worldview, our moral compass and everything!

WHAT DO WE SEE?

In this light, what do we see? Do we see darkness and evil in the world? Let's pray for God's light and life to influence and invade whatever challenges we face, whether in the workplace, finances, family, relationships, illness or spiritual life. Can we pray for that light and life to make a difference in the hearts and lives of those perpetrating and those suffering from the effects of evil and terror, darkness, destruction and death in the world?

Do we see the beauty of Creation? If we do, that's good but even more, do we see the One behind the beauty? Let us worship our Creator. "*Lord, our Lord, how majestic is Your name in all the earth! You have set your glory in the heavens*" (Psalm 8:1) or "*The heavens declare the glory of God, the skies proclaim the work of His hands*" (Psalm 19:1). Glory be to God on high, and to His Name be praise. As it was in the beginning, is now and ever shall be, world without end. Amen.

What we see impacts how we can make the most of life—or not. Where we start makes a difference in how we view ourselves, the people around us, and humanity in general. Once again, the Bible has a lot to say, starting at the beginning.

Questions

How would you answer the following arguments from atheists?

- Seeking meaning in life from someone else, like God, is infantile. True fullness and meaning is found in what we make it.

- Faith is an excuse to escape from thinking and facing scientific evidence.

- The universe as observed has none of the qualities considered so important to Bible believers: it has no design, no purpose, no evil, no good, no meaning.

How does the biblical world view differ from the evolutionary view of struggle where only the fittest survive while the weak are expendable?

Discuss this idea: Rather than being scientific, atheism is inconsistent with the scientific method because it makes a categorical statement that expresses belief in non-belief.

What is the live-giving starting point of your day? How about the starting point of a week? How does God make a difference to this?

CHAPTER 2

In the Beginning, Man

As we have seen, the main character of Genesis, and the whole of the Bible, is God. The next characters to appear are mankind or humanity, created by God and crowned with glory, to be dwellers and managers of this Creation.

Unfortunately, things get off to a shaky start. Just as we are wondering where this world is going and how we people fit in, we see that people have two very different paths before us. They divide truth and untruth, life and death. As in our view of God, these differing paths affect our worldview and values, our personal and social choices, our moral and ethical compass. They form the basis for the hot-button moral and ethical dilemmas facing us today. If we grasp the truth of verses in Genesis 3, we will better understand what is happening around us, and receive a foundation for making, healthy, godly, and righteous choices.

THE MORAL DILEMMA

Let me begin by clarifying the meaning of two words. Morality comes from the Latin word *mos* or mores, meaning custom, and is a description of "what is," the acceptable custom in a particular group or culture. Ethics comes from the word *ethos*, meaning character, and is concerned with what ought to be. Ethics presents a higher standard. When we do away with an external or absolute standard, we often replace it with the standard of what is regarded as normal and acceptable by society. A populist morality determines the ethical standard, instead of the other way round. This is what we see today as moral choices have been framed as human rights issues rather than referencing biblical ethical values.

How does the Bible fit into this dilemma? From Genesis, we can see two starting points based on two different viewpoints:

GOD'S VIEW

Genesis 2:16, 17 says, "*And the* L*ORD* *God commanded the man, 'You are free to eat from any tree in the garden but you must not eat from the tree of the knowledge of good and evil for when you eat from it you will surely die.'*" This offers an external objective absolute standard. God gives a provision and a prohibition. God gives by His grace, blesses us in abundance, makes provision to meet our every need but within this provision, He also gives prohibitions and restraints, setting boundaries, which are for our own good. There are consequences for our actions ("*For when you eat from it, you will surely die*").

We often confuse two aspects of God, His truth and His love. Some think love negates prohibitions. Others are so focused on truth that they trip over love and fall into the trap of legalism. Jesus sets Himself as the standard, "*I am the way and the truth and the life*" (John 14:6). He summarizes the Old Testament commandments and laws under the banner of loving God and loving our neighbour, equating love with obedience. "*If you love me, keep my commands*" (John 14:15). Love and truth are two sides of the same coin.

THE WORLD'S VIEW

The way the world views love and truth is different. All the new spiritualities and moralities question standards, values and obedience. They want the spiritual feel-good without the commands and prohibitions which they regard as outdated killjoys. For many, love means accepting everything and doing as you please. Of course, there is nothing new under the sun, and we can see this early in the next chapter in Genesis.

"*Did God really say…?*" (Genesis 3:2) asks that old con artist, the serpent who questions and doubts God's Word followed by the real kicker, the total deception: "*…When you eat from it, your eyes will be opened, and you will be like God, knowing good and evil*" (Genesis 3:5).

This worldview is determined not by God, but by self. In effect self is deified; self decides what is right and what is wrong. This is the essence of the word "sin."

We fall short of God's standards by imposing our own—I did it my way! This sinful self then sets the standard which can't help but be flawed.

Even more serious, when God is questioned, ignored, disobeyed and replaced with self, we can see the result, a descent into chaos, immorality and tragedy, not just individually, but as a society. At one time, there was an attempt to base social values on the former God-view. In particular, the Ten Commandments were used as a standard for moral and social order. What do we see in our society today? It is God's commandments that are becoming prohibited. Adultery and promiscuity have become normative, while virginity before marriage is ridiculed. Endless advertising seeks to use greed and envy to promote consumerism and accumulation of more and more, bigger and better, for me and mine. This contributes to violence, crime, murder and mayhem. From petty thieves to organized crime, stealing is less about taking something really needed, such as food for survival, and more about satisfying selfish appetites. All are a direct consequence of eliminating God from personal and public consciousness.

What do we see? With what lens do we see? What do we do with what we see? The Bible tells us what Adam and Eve saw and then did. *"When the woman saw that the fruit of the tree was good for food and pleasing to the eye,…she took some and ate it. She also gave some to her husband, who was with her, and he ate it"* (Genesis 3:6). This ignored the fact that it wasn't hers to give.

How sin is birthed and conceived is not rocket science. Seeing leads to action—taking and eating. James confirms how this works: *"But each person is tempted when they are dragged away by their own evil desire and enticed. Then, after desire has conceived, it gives birth to sin; and sin, when it is full-grown, gives birth to death"* (James 1:14, 15). One famous example of this can be seen in King David's seduction of Bathsheba. *"One evening David got up from his bed and walked around… from the roof he saw a woman bathing. The woman was very beautiful,… Then David sent messengers to get her. She came to him, and he slept with her"* (2 Samuel 11:2-4).

He saw, he sent, he slept with her. He satisfied and rationalized his desire, which gave birth to sin.

What we view is also related to choices and consequences. Back in Eden, Satan's false claim was that *"Your eyes will be opened, and you will be like God."* But what did Adam and Eve actually see? The Bible says, *"Then the eyes of both of them were opened, and they realized they were naked; so they…made coverings for themselves"* (Genesis 3:7). Instead of seeing like God, they saw themselves and one another naked, becoming self-conscious rather than God-conscious.

With every choice, there is a consequence. For the woman, the consequence of the Fall was that *"with painful labor you will give birth to children"* (Genesis 3:16); the consequence to the man was that, *"by the sweat of your brow you will eat your food"* (Genesis 3:19). And for humankind, the consequence was banishment from the Garden of Eden and separation from the One who is the source of life (Genesis 3:23).

This failure sets the context for our existence. The consequence of the Fall for humanity was pain and exclusion from God's presence. The whole of the universe spun out of harmony with the Creator. The good news is that God doesn't leave us in this desolation. God has a plan, summed up in one word: redemption.

Dysfunctional humanity has all too often practiced a different way of responding. Instead of recognizing sin and making amends, we cover it up as Adam and Eve clothed themselves in fig leaves. It is the same story over and over again. We rationalize, deny, and ignore, hoping our mistakes will go away; we pass the buck and blame someone else. Adam not only blames Eve, he even blames God — *"The woman you put here with me...she gave me..."* (Genesis 3:12). Eve blames the serpent, and the serpent didn't have a leg to stand on. Okay, that's a joke. But this isn't: in our pride, we cover up sin with excuses.

MODERN MORALITY

These verses set the scene for ethical issues today. It is my hope to set out a template on how to navigate these waters by following the principles of recognizing God as Creator and God's authority over our lives.

How do the words, *"God said..."* impact our choices? One of the hot-button issues of today, one of life and death, can be seen in the question of whether we should be pro-choice or pro-life. We ask this question both around whether we have the right to choose to end life in the unborn, and whether we can take life by medically assisted suicide.

There is very real pain and suffering in these kinds of situations. I empathize with women who are faced with an unwanted pregnancy. Many are scared and hurting. For those facing terminal illnesses, the thought of becoming incapacitated can be too much to handle. Others are living with terrible physical pain. We should not take lightly or even claim to understand all that they are going through.

But God has something to say about these complex questions. What are some of the factors at play here? We see two perspectives on humanity: on the one hand, we are created in the image of God and reflect His character (Genesis

1:27). On the other, we are sinful, self-centred human beings who fall short of God's standards :"*For all have sinned and fall short of the glory of God*" (Romans 3:23). We do reflect both sides—the great qualities of God and the worst of human nature.

We also have different kinds of life in us. One is biological, physical, dust of the ground, "*Then the Lord God formed a man from the dust of the ground*" (Genesis 2:7). At the same time, we have the breath of life: "*The Lord…breathed into his nostrils the breath of life, and the man became a living being*" (Genesis 2:7).

PRO-CHOICE OR PRO-LIFE

What does this say in relation to the pro-choice or pro-life argument? In instances of rape, incest, medical danger to the mother and such complex issues, I believe there needs to be a conversation between the woman, her family, medical staff, spiritual advisors and God. God gives us free will, and therefore we have the freedom to make choices.

Abortion has euphemistically been called a woman's reproductive right. No mention is made of responsibilities, which go hand in hand with any rights.

I will say that that a couple who is listening to God's directives makes choices when they choose to have sex and when they decide on birth control. God designed sex to take place within the confines of marriage.

The reproductive rights of women are rationalized by pro-choice advocates to the exclusion of the human life in the womb. Someone has said that the place where a baby should be safest, in their mother's womb, is now one of the most dangerous.

Here is how the decision is rationalized. If we are convinced that the unborn is not human, but simply some fetal tissue, then it can be discarded at will. Some activists go to great lengths to save a tree or a whale while discarding an unborn human being as disposable tissue.

To me, the inconsistency, deception, and lack of logic in this thinking would be laughable if it were not so tragic. It is a simple choice of believing a lie that leads to death, or a truth which gives life.

Many Bible verses show God's view, but one is particularly poignant. It was a baby in the womb who first rejoiced at news of Mary's conception of Jesus:

When Elizabeth heard Mary's greeting, the baby leaped in her womb, and Elizabeth was filled with the Holy Spirit. In a loud voice she exclaimed, 'Blessed are you among women, and blessed is the child you will bear!...As

...oon as the sound of your greeting reached my ears, the baby in my womb leaped for joy." (Luke 1:41, 42, 44)

CHOICES

When we make moral choices, where we start determines our conclusion. When we fall for the lie that says, *"Did God really say?"*, the natural starting point of our worldview is "in the beginning, me." This forms the basis for why I express and demand my rights, my needs, my way, my life, my truth. A direct consequence is believing, "It's my body, don't tell me what to do with what is mine." We deify ourselves, believing our life is our own to do with as we please, giving ourselves the right to decide when we can take life. The deception is ingrained in our contemporary society.

Since the infamous Roe v. Wade decision in 1973, abortion has been legal in the USA. The irony is that "Jane Roe" as she was called completely changed her position on abortion when she became a Christian. As a pro-life activist, Norma McCorvey (Jane Roe's real name) said her involvement in the court case was "the biggest mistake in my life."[2] I recently watched the movie, *Unplanned,* which tells the story of Abby Johnson, the youngest director of Planned Parenthood, which offers reproductive health services, including abortions. After seeing firsthand the horror of what actually happen to babies during abortion, Johnson completely reversed her position and became an anti-abortion, pro-life activist.

When we cut the Creator out of the equation, we can rationalize and justify anything. When we start with God, then the choice of how we see our bodies is very different. Paul warns: *"Do you not know that your bodies are temples of the Holy Spirit, who is in you, whom you have received from God? You are not your own; you were bought at a price. Therefore honor God with your bodies"* (1 Corinthians 6:19-20). God's Word affirms that right from conception, God is both Creator and Giver of life: *"For You created my inmost being; You knit me together in my mother's womb. I praise You because I am fearfully and wonderfully made"* (Psalm 139:13,14). God's view leads to a belief in the sanctity of life, knowing that we will answer to Him for usurping His place and taking what we have no right to take.

LIFE OR DEATH

These two ways are a choice between life or death — literally, light or darkness, truth or untruth, God's way or our way. Jesus had quite a lot to say about truth, and love. As we have seen, they are closely connected.

[2] McCorvey, Norma. "Norma McCorvey Of Roe v. Wade Embodied The Complexity Of American Abortion Debate", All Things Considered, NPR, February 18, 2017.

Love doesn't mean doing what we please. This reality is well illustrated by two words very much in vogue today: tolerance and inclusion. Critics see the concept of a God who judges as unloving. However, we also see those who advocate for tolerance being extremely intolerant of anything with which they don't agree. We have universities refusing to allow speakers who disagree with their left wing agenda, gay pride marches excluding police, restaurant owners kicking out a government party on moral grounds, and a law society challenging the license of a Christian university that upholds a biblical view of sex and marriage. Few of these moral police realize that one day they too will stand before Jesus and will have to answer for every thought, feeling, action and behaviour, not to mention their judgments. Only this time it will be on His terms and according to His standards. What society decides is tolerant or intolerant does not necessarily line up with God's view.

I do want to say that over the years I have counselled and prayed with many women going through experiences after abortions. One was an elderly woman who was still deeply distraught because of an abortion when she was young. Another was a very active Christian who confessed to having two abortions. The serenity prayer offers wisdom. There are things we cannot change, but we can take responsibility and have the courage to change the things we can, and we need wisdom to know the difference. We prayed together and invited Jesus into that past hurt, receiving his forgiveness and healing. We entrusted that unborn life to the Lord. I don't know how God will sort out this mess in eternity, but I do know that God is in the redemption business. His intention is to bring light out of darkness, life from death, and hope from suffering. Nothing is too hard for Him.

He can redeem and restore, renew and recreate what is broken or lost. We don't come in pride, dictating our rights and opinions. We come to Him in humility and confession to receive His forgiveness and salvation, His comfort and counsel, His healing and peace. This was my hope for these women, starting from the position that God was in the beginning.

Jesus invites everyone to follow Him, but when we do, we discover that this doesn't mean doing what we please, doing things my way. God does not tolerate sin; He defines the terms of what is acceptable to Him or not.

How can we line up with His standard? Jesus is clear in his very direct call, *"Repent for the kingdom of God has come near...follow me"* (Matthew 4:17,19). Repent means to turn around or change; it doesn't mean that we can just continue with our own choices and direction. This requires obedience to His ways and commands; it means a complete transfer of allegiance. *"For He has rescued us from the dominion of darkness and brought us into the kingdom of the Son He loves, in whom we have redemption, the forgiveness of sins"* (Colossians 1:13, 14). When we belong to one kingdom, the other doesn't make sense. So we should not be surprised when the world hates what we stand for. Jesus says, *"If the world hates you, keep in mind that it hated me…If they persecuted Me, they will also persecute you also…They will treat you this way because of my name, for they do not know the one who sent me"* (John 15:18, 20, 21). Jesus earlier says of the Holy Spirit, *"The world cannot accept him, because it neither sees him nor knows him. But you know him for he lives with you and will be in you"* (John 14:17). The Holy Spirit advocates on our behalf as the Spirit of truth. He exposes the shallow self-serving agenda of our sinful nature. Here is the real choice which faces everyone: to continue following our own way which leads to death, or follow God's way, which leads to life.

The point from where we start affects our worldview and values, our personal and social choices, our moral and ethical compass, and ultimately, where we end up. One thing is true for all of us, we begin our journey in this life at a certain time, and it ends at a certain time. We have little control over the when, but we can take responsibility for what we do and how to make the most of the time in between those two points.

Questions

In a world where "fake news" is the buzzword, how can we tell truth from untruth?

Do you think people are intrinsically good or evil?

What is the actual basis for the way we make decisions? Describe what gives a moral compass and how that impacts our day-to-day choices?

We live in a world that seems to ignore or is openly hostile to God's view. Can you give a reason why you believe?

Read through Psalm 139 carefully and prayerfully.
Pray:

Lord, we pray for all those who have been hurt by decisions they have made, decisions we have made. Fill us with Your love and compassion.

We pray for our aging and ailing saints, that they might not lose heart, but know that while outwardly we are wasting away, inwardly we are being renewed day by day.

Lord, keep our eyes fixed on You the author and perfecter of our faith.

Lord we stand on Your Word, we follow You Lord Jesus, the Way the Truth and the Life. Come Holy Spirit and help us to be obedient servants. We pray for the Church.

We stand for life from the womb to the grave, from the first breath to the last, and thank You Lord for giving us Your gift of life.

We give thanks that we are fearfully and wonderfully made, and You are transforming us more and more into Your image.

We pray for the world, and those who are caught in the deceptions of the evil one.

Lord God, this is the day that You have made, we will rejoice in it and be glad. Holy Spirit, breathe new life into us that we will make the most of every moment.

Hear these words of comfort our Saviour Christ says to all who truly turn to Him:

"Come to me, all you who are weary and burdened, and I will give you rest" (Matthew 11.28).

"For God so loved the world that He gave His one and only Son, that whoever believes in Him shall not perish but have eternal life" (John 3:16).

"Here is a trustworthy saying that deserves full acceptance: Christ Jesus came into the world to save sinners" (1 Timothy 1:15).

"If anybody does sin, we have an Advocate with the Father—Jesus Christ, the Righteous One. He is the atoning sacrifice for our sins" (1 John 2:1, 2).

CHAPTER 3
Redeeming Our Time

G od is in the redemption business. This means He takes the elements of decay, corruption and loss associated with our imperfect, fallen world, and restores them to His perfect will and purpose. Unfortunately time is one such element that—once lost—is gone forever. Or is it?

Wouldn't it be nice if we could get control over time? We could recapture lost opportunities, make up for mistakes, and recover our youth. The benefits would be endless. Hollywood has played with this notion in movies like *Groundhog Day* where the protagonist has to live the same twenty-four hours over and over until he learns the lesson of doing good to others, and in particular how to selflessly love his lady. While we can't literally turn back time, there are ways to recover from past mishaps.

Remembrance of special days are another way of capturing moments in time. Nations observe historical events with special holidays. We enjoy celebrating important personal milestones in our lives—birthdays, anniversaries, and other significant occasions. Besides giving opportunity for celebration and thanksgiving, these are moments to reflect on what we have done and are doing with our time. The admonition to remember is repeated again and again in the Bible. God knows our propensity to forget. In our Judeo-Christian heritage, we set aside days to remember what God has done for us.

Two Greek words for time are used in the Bible. *Chronos* is the concept of time which is linear, with a beginning and an end. Events are moving towards a conclusion, rather than an ongoing cycle. Within this chronology there is *kairos,* particular God-appointed moments of decision and opportunity. In relation to eternity, our lifespan is but a moment. The psalmist says, "*Yet you sweep people away in the sleep of death—they are like the new grass of the morning: in the morning it springs up new, but by evening it is dry and withered*" (Psalm 90:5,6).

CHRONOS TIME

One minute we are waking up, and the next it is time to go to bed. One day we are rejoicing in the life of a newborn baby in the family, and the next those babies have grown up, are married and having babies of their own. One moment we are looking to our parents for nurture, provision and protection while the next we are making that provision for them, and soon enough mourning their passing. One day a person may be full of life, and the next cold, dead and gone. That sounds so depressing, especially as time moves on relentlessly and starts to run out on us, and we find ourselves deeper and deeper into the second half, third period, last quarter, depending on which sport one follows. Yet, God is sovereign and the author of life and death. "*All the days ordained for me were written in Your book before one of them came to be*" (Psalm 139:16).

We say glibly that life is a gift but that is the truth. Life is given to us for a short while as our privilege and responsibility, to do with as we will in the time we have allotted. So what are we doing with this gift of time? "I am too busy," we say, when what we really mean is that something is not a priority for us at the moment. We all have twenty-four hours of time, but we have choices to make the best of each moment. Once again God's Word gives us perspective and wisdom. The psalmist says, "*Teach us to number our days, that we may gain a heart of wisdom*" (Psalm 90:12). Paul warns, "*Be very careful, then, how you live — not as unwise but as wise, making the most of every opportunity, because the days are evil*" (Ephesians 5:15-16).

This last declaration—"*because the days are evil*"— is thrown in as though we should understand what it means. We have already introduced the reality of an evil power, the serpent from Genesis 3, or Satan. In the Bible, he is described in many different ways. One that fits this context is, "*the god of this age [who] has blinded the minds of unbelievers*" (2 Corinthians 4:4). Every age is blinded by untruth, fed by the devil, described as "*a liar and the father of lies*" (John 8:44), who "*himself masquerades as an angel of light*" (2 Corinthians 11:14). The spirit of the age may make sense to ears and eyes influenced by the values and perceptions of the day but offers worthless counsel against the constancy of God's truth.

How do we know the difference? We measure everything against that which doesn't sway with every breeze of the moment. Everything we know with our senses is transitory and will pass away (Matthew 24:35). As we have already seen, God's eternal nature is revealed all the way through His Word. From God being the beginning of all things to the declaration of His identity in the encounter with Moses, *"I Am Who I Am"* (Exodus 3:14), to some of our core descriptions of Jesus Christ Himself: *"I am the Alpha and the Omega…who is, and who was, and who is to come, the Almighty* (Revelation 1:8).

SEASONS AND CYCLES

God's purposes are revealed in His Word and all around us. He speaks to us through the seasons and cycles of life. Ecclesiastes 3, made famous by the sixties pop group the Byrds in the song "Turn, Turn, Turn," reminds us there is a season for everything.

Nature reveals the seasons, each with their own specific purpose. For farmers and gardeners, spring is for sowing, summer for tending new shoots, fall is for harvesting the crop, and winter for pruning, reviewing, and preparation for the next year.

Pruning is an important part of producing a productive plant. Cutting away superfluous parts that waste resources releases life to new buds coming into bloom. This principle applies to spiritual life as well, as given by Jesus Himself:

> *I am the true vine, and my Father is the gardener. He cuts off every branch in me that bears no fruit, while every branch that does bear fruit, He prunes so that it will be even more fruitful…Remain in me, as I also remain in you"* (John 15:1, 2, 4).

Reviewing ministry over forty years I see seasons of growth unrelated to anything we were doing but initiated by a sovereign move of the Holy Spirit. There were times of review and preparation leading to pruning, change with endings and new beginnings. Then there were times of consolidation, nurturing and tending what had begun. In my personal life and church ministry, dealing with events that seemed overwhelming, impossible or failed could have led to my giving up. Sadly, for a variety of reasons, attrition among pastors is very high. Instead, these challenges can be seen as opportunities for pruning, perseverance and discovering new opportunities. When I faced leaving the security of ministry in an established church and planting a new congregation, I found God releasing me from fear as I learned to rest and trust in Him as my provider and protector.

RESTORING WHAT IS LOST

Jesus is Lord of the history of the ages and our personal history. While we are stuck in the moment, He can transcend any circumstance, recovering and redeeming that which has been lost. *"I will repay you for the years the locusts have eaten"* (Joel 2:25). I have experienced God's redemption firsthand in many different ways. I shared some of these stories in a previous book, but they are worth repeating.

I see one example in my academic career. I did not apply myself to studies and was a mediocre student until the Lord became my professor. He taught me discipline, giving me a love of learning and improved grades that saw me end up with degrees and diplomas, including a scholarship opportunity that led to a doctorate. All of it was a gift of God's grace, to which I had to respond in faith combined with hard work.

Another emerged during our experience of becoming parents. While we were at college in England, Lynne began to show signs of pregnancy but there was no life growing in her womb. One day she was rushed to hospital in acute pain; it was discovered she had an ectopic pregnancy, with the fetus growing in one of her Fallopian tubes. She ended up losing the child for which we had longed, along with Fallopian tube and one ovary. The other tube was also blocked with a latent ectopic pregnancy and so we were told our chances of conceiving were extremely low. One possibility that offered a fifteen per cent possibility of future pregnancy was to surgically insert a plastic tube in place of the damaged tube. The night before Lynne went in for this operation, we broke bread and knelt in prayer before the Lord. After she came out of the anesthetic, the surgeon reported there had been no need for the replacement as the tube was already open. When asked for an explanation, his response was, "It's one of those things only the Good Lord knows." It was seven years before our son was born, but we knew the Lord had redeemed the years of waiting and struggling as He gave us this desire of our heart. As a bonus, we were blessed with two beautiful daughters as well.

The Lord our God can and does turn back even the clock when it suits His purpose to bless us beyond our imagination.

LIVING FOR TODAY

So often we live with regrets for past mistakes and failures, worrying about what may or may not happen in the future, and failing to enjoy or make the most of our present reality. Then one day we wake up to find that our lives have slipped away and we wonder what we have accomplished. Jesus tells us not to worry about tomorrow, but to live in the reality of today (Matthew 6:34). He is also Lord of our future, and promises: *"Never will I leave you; never will I forsake you"* (Hebrews 13:5). We have been given a glimpse into the future through apocalyptic (meaning hidden) Scripture like what we read in the book of Revelation. But the reality is that we can entrust all our uncertainties, anxieties and cares to the One who holds our future in His very capable hands. It is not what we know but Who.

As a parent and now grandparent, I see how children completely entrust their lives to their parents. They don't know where they are being taken, where their next meal is coming from, or what dangers may face them. But if they are with their parents, that is all the assurance they need.

My wife and I are called special names by our grandchildren. Lynne is Nana. In the Bible there is a term that describes a personal, loving relationship we have with God our Heavenly Father. *"…the Spirit you received brought about your adoption to sonship. And by Him we cry, 'Abba, Father!'"* (Romans 8:15) *Abba* can also be used as a term of affection, endearment, and respect for an elder person—like a grandfather. Why, I am not sure, but our eldest granddaughter started calling me Abba when she was very young. I have become Abba to all my grandchildren, and I love it.

I remember a few years ago, playing with our eldest grandchild in a swimming pool; she was learning to jump off the side. At first it was "Too far, Abba." But as she grew in confidence, knowing I was there to catch her, she was happy to jump farther and farther. Likewise, if we have our hand in the hand of our Heavenly Father, our *Abba,* that is all we need to trust Him with our past, present and future. This includes our long-term future, where He is Lord of Eternity and holds the keys to eternal life, and for those pivotal *kairos* moments when He comes into such sharp focus.

Questions

When we say that we are too busy, what are we really saying?

How can we make the most of the twenty-four hours of each *chronos* day? Is there a better way to make the most of *kairos* moments?

Review your personal and ministry life in the light of seasons and cycles. What can you see? What are some of the benefits of pruning…abiding…. resting….reviewing…?

Discuss what these verses mean to you.: Psalm 90:12; Joel 2:25; Psalm 118:24.

How can they give a sense of purpose as we live out the days numbered for us?

Work through this personal exercise on how to make the most of our time.

- Ensure that we are at peace with our past and future.
- Commit the beginning of each day to the Lord and seek His direction.
- In the short term, learn to focus on the tasks at hand. Set our goals in writing, prioritize them, and then get them done.
- Have a long-term vision. Where would we like to be and what would we like to accomplish by this time next year…in five, ten years?
- See every person, situation, and even interruption which confronts us as a *kairos* God-moment where we are His representative to accomplish His purpose.
- Recognize that there are different phases in our lives, each of which offers new challenges and opportunities. As we get older, we may not be able to lift, run and jump like we did as youngsters, but our experience and maturity opens different doors.
- Never be afraid to try new things, be flexible and ready to learn. There is nothing more restricting than a know-it-all who is set in his ways.

- Be ready to take hold of the opportunities that unfold before us and don't allow cold feet to rob us of God's best. *Carpe Diem*—seize the day!
- Ask the Lord to help us grow into maturity rather than just growing old.
- Trust the Lord as the One who does hold our life, our past, present and our future in His hands.
- Have such faith in Jesus, that our reality is centred in Him rather than our own existence. Then we can say with Paul, *"For me to live is Christ, and to die is gain"* (Philippians 1:21)
- Accept that today is the day and this is the year that the Lord has made, and we will make the most of each moment as we rejoice and are glad in it.

CHAPTER 4

Making the Most of Life's Stages

One of the insights that makes aging so much more meaningful is the way *kairos* moments intersect with *chronos* time. Within our lifespan, we experience different stages, each of which has its challenges and blessings, drawbacks and opportunities. There is no constant upward mobile trajectory. It goes up and down, but we can *"number our days"* (Psalm 90:12). God introduces us in Genesis to themes that help us understand ourselves and our lives.

Within these different stages, each day is a gift we can embrace as we rejoice and make the most of every opportunity. We can live today to the fullest. We can learn from the past without being tied to our mistakes. We can look forward without being sidelined by wishful thinking. A healthy view of our past and future helps us to make the most of this day. I want to look at several thematic areas in which I have embraced God's activity in my life at different stages: formation, consolidation, tribulation, restoration, and retirement.

FORMATION

The Spirit of God brought form and fullness out of the void at Creation—*"Now the earth was formless and empty…and the Spirit of God was hovering over the waters"* (Genesis 1:2). He does the same with each of us. From conception through birth, childhood, adolescence and adulthood, throughout our entire life, we are in a process of formation.

I grew up in a fairly normal, imperfectly happy home in Durban, South Africa. I was baptized as a child with my parents sincerely intending to offer me to God and raise me in His ways. My primary school education was happy and successful as I did moderately well at school, loved all kinds of sports, excelled at a few, and was elected a prefect. My transition to high school never quite lived up to my expectations. I managed but did not excel academically and participated in many sports, but on the whole, I did not enjoy being there. Low points included facing a bully who chose me to pick on. (It was only when I stood up to him—I have a chipped tooth as a reminder of my trouble—that he never bothered me again.) This was an incentive for me to get self-defense training, but since then I have never raised my fists to anyone.

My first year at university continued in the same fairly mundane manner until things deteriorated into turmoil, failure and confusion. I decided that the best way of being educated was to travel around the world and "find myself." After hitchhiking around Zimbabwe (or Rhodesia as it was known then), I discovered the world was bigger than I thought. I was turned back at the Zambia border and headed into Johannesburg as an impressionable twenty-one-year-old hippy who could have gone any number of directions. These years of youthful energy and zeal could have been accompanied by indiscretion and even danger but I see the hand of God in them as He not only protected me from taking a wrong turn on the road, but led me to young folk who looked and spoke like I did, with long hair, Levi's jeans, and punctuating every sentence with "beautiful" or "man." But unlike me, they spoke about Jesus as if they actually knew Him.

One Saturday night, I found myself in a prayer meeting. I received prayer but nothing particular happened. Later we were praying again—twice in one night—when I had a profound sense of peace and holy presence. At one in the morning, I found myself in deep prayer and speaking in a language I didn't understand. It was like I was being filled with the very presence of God. I had a personal encounter with Jesus Christ. I was filled to overflowing with the Holy Spirit. My journey as a follower of Jesus Christ had begun.

CONSOLIDATION

In early adulthood, most young folk are being trained and heading onto their career path, getting married and having children, and looking for their first home. There are all sorts of variations on these pathways and all the boxes will not be ticked by everyone but generally these are part of what I see as the theme of consolidation.

I moved back to Durban where God began to re-form and consolidate me as a disciple of Christ. I knew little more than that I had been told to give up smoking and to go to church. I did that immediately, was led to a church, and then had to decide what to do with my life. I found a job in administration at the airport that allowed me to attend university classes in the evening and complete my degree under the Lord's tutelage. With a daily discipline and routine, I also discovered a love of learning, reading and studying, which in turn was accompanied by growing academic achievement.

Another aspect of my life began to consolidate although the seeds were planted before my hitchhiking trip. Lynne and I had met at a university ball, although we were with different partners. We hit it off and spent a lot of time chatting to each other. The next weekend, I found an excuse to go to her house to ask for the address of my friend who was her partner, even though I actually already knew it. I discovered she was in a convent praying whether to become a nun. She heard God say that He had other things in store for her. When she arrived home, her mother told her that a long-haired character had come to see her. I then phoned to invite her out. It happened to be Easter weekend. She turned me down on Maundy Thursday, Good Friday, and Easter Saturday, because she was going to church. I figured Sunday was a bust and wondered if she was a religious nut but I decided to give it one more try. On Easter Monday, she finally accepted. Being the romantic I am, we went to the motor races along with three of my buddies for moral support.

Lynne applied for and received an American Field Scholarship that took her to West Covina, California, USA, for a year. We missed each other, wrote frequent letters and enjoyed a great reunion on her return. But after three months, this rather reserved South African boy and her newly acquired Americanisms did not get on too well. We broke up. This was when I went on my hitchhiking trip, was soundly converted, and realized I was not over her. To make a long story short, God reunited us, and Lynne and I were married December 16, 1972.

Added to the mix, I had a growing sense that I was being called by the Lord to serve in ministry. I became more involved in church activities, leading a newcomers Bible study and serving on the leadership.

We then set off for three years' theological training at St. John's College and the University of Nottingham, England. Living in residence and being fully involved in college life was an excellent experience preparing us for ministry.

It wasn't easy relating to so many different personalities, cultures, and talented people, and I only learned to appreciate the benefits of this time after facing similar challenges in day-to-day church ministry. (Most of those of us who went through class together have kept in touch all these years and enjoyed a wonderful forty-year reunion in September 2017.)

As a bonus, this one-time mediocre student was given the opportunity to do graduate studies. I applied to Fuller Theological Seminary in Pasadena, California, USA, and my growing confidence combined with perseverance, powered by God's grace, resulted in my acceptance into the School of Theology with a full scholarship as well as a bursary to pay for travel, and a gift from my church to provide for books. While continuing my church ministry, I was able to pursue studies at Fuller, reading, writing assignments and attending seminars at the Pasadena campus, before completing a dissertation and graduating with a Doctor of Ministry.

I was ordained July 31, 1977. God took my mixed-up life—education, career, relationships, emotions, thoughts, indecisions and spiritual meandering—and put my feet firmly on His foundation of stability, clarity, purpose and overall consolidation. We settled in Durban where I served as an assistant pastor at Christchurch, Addington for just over two years, before becoming the Rector of St. Augustine's Church, Queensburgh. This was described as a non-viable parish, but we saw God move in Holy Spirit renewal to grow a vibrant church including what would be my first building project.

Our family life was also consolidating. As mentioned, God had redeemed our initial problems in having children. Life seemed good, but I was about to go through a steep new learning curve.

TRIBULATION

Just when everything seems to be running smoothly, something can happen which derails all those good intentions. Starting right doesn't mean that everything runs in a straight line. We see this in Genesis when God said to Adam and Eve, "*Cursed...pains in childbearing...through painful toil...by the sweat of your brow...for dust you are and to dust you will return.*" (Genesis 3:14, 16, 19). It is also true for us today. Crises can hit us at any age. Illness, injury, unemployment, bankruptcy, financial hardships, relationship breakdown, failure, addictions, divorce, children going off the rails, death—these are all issues people have to face. We can wonder if there is more to life than what we have seen so far. This is a danger point when we can make wrong choices with serious consequences.

It was in our midlife years that we faced a number of challenges, many of which were unexpected. When we moved to a new church in Cape Town, in the midst of Lynne's health issues, things went from bad to worse. After just over a year I was faced with something that challenged my core. One of our leaders was living in a same-sex relationship, saw nothing wrong with the situation, and came very vocally out of the closet. This was over thirty years ago when people didn't really talk about such things as much. I challenged whether someone in a practising same-sex relationship should be in a leadership position. Things got ugly, and I ended up resigning from a ministry I had worked so hard to build, leaving with no job, no income, no house, and three young children. Our lives were turned upside down as we bounced from consolidation to chaos. The good news was I discovered a walk in the wilderness is often God's way of refining us and teaching us to depend completely on Him. Whatever the life-changing surprises we have to deal with, we can choose to treat them as God's way to fulfill His promises.

We ended up planting Kingsway Christian Fellowship with a small group who gathered around us to pray with us. We started meeting in a house, moved into a church building where services were at a less than convenient time, before ending up in a school. The school location meant dealing with the weekly inconvenience of moving furniture, setting up music equipment, and having to clean up before and after services. However, we saw the Lord's blessing in a relatively short time.

The Breadbasket ministry was just one instance of God's blessing. I regularly drove past an area where men from two townships on the outskirts of Cape Town came to wait for a day of work. The Lord spoke to me and said, "What are you doing for the Lazaruses on your doorstep?" That was a shocker! Casual labourers used to hang out on the streets, forcing window-washing on motorists stopped at traffic lights. We began to spend time getting to know these men, providing food with no strings attached, serving and relating. I was aware of the danger of do-gooders who preach at people and then give up. It took a year of building trust before things started to happen. They began to ask questions: why were we there? where was our church situated? Would I say grace for the meal? One day we prayed for someone with a broken leg and he was healed. Slowly, these men began to come to church. One day, seven men committed their lives and were baptized. Many began to come and ask for prayer for work. Against all odds, people found work. Thanks to the generosity of a businessman, others were given scholarships for an opportunity to learn a trade. God enriched our church as we came to represent the incredible diversity of South African society—black and white, rich and poor, old and young.

Those from the poor township communities surrounding the more affluent Cape Town taught us so much. They would hold all-night prayer and worship meetings. When they shared their testimonies at church, we wondered how these simple men knew so much, yet we could see they had met Jesus. One day a colleague and I were at one of the house groups. When we were ready to go, we discovered that the house was surrounded by a drunken mob who were ready to harm us. Our hosts managed to get us out safely by talking with the mob. On another occasion, I had the sad responsibility of going into the townships to take the funeral of one of our own who had been killed when his house was burned down. It was a glorious testimony to this beleaguered community.

It is key that we take each lesson from difficult battles and use them as building blocks to the next one. The lessons learned here stood us in good stead for our next adventure a few years later.

Just as we were getting back on our feet and consolidating, our lives were once again turned upside down. It was probably be more accurate to say our lives were turned downside up as we accepted a call to a church on the other side of the world, emigrating to Canada. When we left to follow our call to Canada, we were blessed with an overwhelming outpouring of love. In God's grace I was able to leave our fellowship in the care of a fellow pastor and friend.

RESTORATION

Ideally we come through the crisis part of midlife and settle into the contentment and fulfillment part. By this stage of life, perhaps the fourth quarter, we will have hopefully gained some wisdom and have learned the principle of passing on what we know to others. As the psalmist says, *"Even when I am old and gray, do not forsake me, my God, till I declare Your power to the next generation"* (Psalm 71:18). In His interaction with Abram in particular, and His people in general, God declares His will. He is the One who creates, authors, perfects, sanctifies, edifies and sustains us in accordance with His purpose. No matter what life stage we are in, we hope to edify those around us, by glorifying and giving pleasure to God. Entering the final chapter of our lives and nearing home, we keep our eyes fixed on the finishing line as we aim to finish well.

One of the verses that kept me going gives us a key to finishing well: *"Let us run with perseverance the race marked out for us, fixing our eyes on Jesus, the pioneer and perfecter of our faith"* (Hebrews 12:1, 2). He shapes our journey as we follow in His footsteps, always more interested in our perfection and completion than our comfort.

RETIREMENT/ OR REDIRECTION.

Before we get to that final resurrection stage, there is one more to add—the big R word. The Bible doesn't mention retirement, but the concept of rest following work is built into the Creation pattern. We can call the time following a life of work, retirement, or it can be a season of redirection in the final period of life. This can be a shaky time; some of God's chosen people made bad mistakes in their latter years, people such as Saul, and even David. Keeping on track with our eyes fixed on the finishing line is a big part of finishing well.

When we are young, we may be upwardly mobile in education, careers, families and homes. Yet there comes a time when we diminish and downsize— physically and mentally—in housing and career, importance and influence. Hopefully, we are also carrying less baggage as we *throw off everything that hinders and the sin that so easily entangles*" (Hebrews 12:1). Paul encourages us: *"Therefore, we do not lose heart. Though outwardly we are wasting away, yet inwardly we are being renewed day by day*" (2 Corinthians 4:16). Part of our preparation to cross the finishing line is this reality: as we become less, Christ becomes more evident as we are being transformed into His likeness.

After I retired, I was often asked how it was going. As I mentioned earlier in this book, I was suddenly hit with a funk. On reflection about why this happened, I realized a number of factors came together. I did not realize just how exhausted I was, and how the years of unrelenting demands and pressures of the ministry had taken their toll. Another factor was that like many of us, I had found my identity in my work. All those years I had been at the centre of all the action, sought out for counsel, fellowship and teaching. Now the phone calls and emails had slowed down to a trickle and had pretty much stopped. Occasional preaching did not satisfy me in the same way as the joy I had found in seeking the Lord for a message to share each week. I no longer had a role. Lynne's health issues did not help and we both lacked the energy and motivation to initiate engagements. On top of that, although I had lots of experience with the behaviour of human beings, I found myself quite disillusioned about the way certain church leaders behaved. I was falling into the old trap of taking my eyes off the author and perfecter of our faith.

During this time, I read a book by E. Stanley Jones called *A Song of Ascents,* which he described as his spiritual autobiography. For him, life was not a struggle but a song. This change came with his conversion, which he described as emancipation from self. In Christ, every struggle is an opportunity to make something out of it, make it serve our life purpose. With this worldview, each life stage is a song of praise as we ascend towards our final destination. Over time, I began to emerge from this funk with a new expectation. The root of the word enthusiasm is *en theos,* literally meaning 'in God.' My enthusiasm began to be restored as I refocused. The Lord gave me a heart for a particular group of pastors who are retired or have been otherwise put out to pasture. For some this has been a painful experience; for others it is just dealing with the natural course of events. I see their experience as a warning for pastors to take the initiative and retire on their own terms, and for churches to show pastoral care and sensitivity. Whatever the form of governance—episcopal, presbyterian, or congregational—we need to value the experience and wisdom of our true elders, pastors who are still serving. I am grateful to the Lord and to my own church that I had the privilege of being able to retire with thanksgiving and joyful celebration. Without the pressure of ministry demands, meetings and agendas, I am learning again to take one step, one person, one day at a time and follow the Lord's direction. This includes getting together weekly with a group of pastors to pray and support one another.

What stage are you in as you read this story? Can you affirm—no matter what you are going through, good, bad, or ugly—that this is the day the Lord has made so we can rejoice and be glad in it? Make the most of every day, every moment, every opportunity, and enjoy the people whom the Lord has given us to come alongside whether that is our spouse, children, grandchildren, family, friends, church family, or brothers and sisters in Christ. May we keep our eyes on the goal of the prize and aim to finish the commission we have been given, steadily working towards the finishing line.

In all things, we give thanks to the Lord for He is good, His love endures forever. In relation to eternity, our lifespan is but a moment. "*You sweep people away in the sleep of death — they are like the new grass of the morning: In the morning it springs up new, but by evening it is dry and withered*" (Psalm 90:5, 6). That may sound rather depressing and hopeless, and yet, "*All the days ordained for me were written in your book before one of them came to be*" (Psalm 139:16).

Before we are swept away by death, how can we become resurrection-ready? How can we grow in maturity rather than just getting older?

Questions

What is the driving force of your life? If it is to serve God's purpose for your generation, and every stage of our lives offers new opportunities, what stage of life are you in now?

Looking back on your own formative years, what were those experiences and influences, people and situations, good, bad and otherwise that shaped your life? Can you invite God into them and affirm the positive or reject the negative?

Where have you seen consolidation? What are the loose ends and areas of unfinished business? Through those ups and downs, ask God to show you His purpose.

What uphill or wilderness battles have you had to face? Did you come out of the battle with a sense of victory of fulfilling God's purpose, or were you more sidetracked? Is it time to invite the Lord to help you get back on track and walk in step with the Holy Spirit?

Whether you are still a way off, approaching, or already in the latter stages of life, what do you need to do today to prepare so that you will finish well? Can you ask God to show you how you can still serve, edify and encourage others?

Can you share your life mission statement in one sentence?

CHAPTER 5

Maturing with Grace

While we have no control over our age, we do have some say over whether we are growing as a person. What does it mean to be mature?

Maturity includes all-round development into the fullness of God's purpose. There is a Hebrew word which is usually interpreted as peace; *shalom* means well-being in every area—physical, emotional, mental, social, relational, economical and spiritual. Likewise, grace is a beautiful word that is the root for many other words packed with meaning, such as graciousness and gracefulness. It comes from a Greek word, *charis*, which literally means unmerited mercy. The qualities of *shalom* and grace come with maturity.

We have seen that part of the aging process involves decreasing while maturity is more about increasing, becoming whole and complete as a person. (If we think we have arrived, that is a good indicator that we haven't.) Growing into maturity is a lifelong journey. How can we be more fruitful, clear-sighted and sure-footed? Maturity requires change and growth, but instead of attrition, it leads to addition!

Once again, our starting point determines our trajectory. God has done his part, giving us all the ingredients we need to grow in wisdom and maturity. He has offered us everything we need for life so that we may participate in His divine nature. This is the key. Do we know and reflect the very nature and characteristics of God Himself? Psalm 139 shows three characteristics of God. He is omniscient (all knowing), omnipresent (present in all places) and omnipotent (all powerful). With such qualities, it is not bad to have God in our corner, no matter what circumstance we face.

CHARACTERISTICS OF GOD

"*You have searched me, Lord, and You know me. You know when I sit and when I rise…Before a word is on my tongue, You, Lord, know it completely*" (Psalm 139:1, 4). God knows our physical location, our thoughts, our path and our journey. He offers His protection—hedging us in, laying His hand upon us. He offers His understanding.

"*You hem me in behind and before, and you lay Your hand upon me*" (Psalm 139:5). God is present with us no matter where we go, the time of day. He is there in the darkness and times of difficulty. He is Emmanuel, God with us. He has made his dwelling among us.

"*For You created my inmost being…your works are wonderful*" (Psalm 139:13, 14). He is all powerful, our Creator God. He has formed us from the moment of our conception so we are fearfully and wonderfully made, as Psalm 139 also declares. Our frame, our substance, and even our future are all fashioned and written in His book.

"*Your hand will guide me, your right hand will hold me fast*" (Psalm 139:10). As we get to know and learn to put our trust in God, we discover that His hand is outstretched to us. What does that mean? We use our hands to carry, guide, protect, lift and bless. This is what we have in relationship with our Heavenly Father. Our future is secure if we put our hand in His hand, following and trusting Him. We discover His hand is reaching out to bless us. As we get to know Him, we discover who we are.

PERSONAL CHARACTERISTICS

Part of growing up involves learning to know our personality. Sadly, today it is even more complicated as folk allow their confusion to become part of their identity. The hot-button issue now is about gender identity. Young kids are being taught that gender is fluid, determined according to their feelings. This takes us back to our view of world and self. When we start with God's view as expressed through his Word, our personal identity is given by Him: "*So God created mankind in his own image…male and female he created them*" (Genesis 1:27). When God is sidelined, self is ultimate, with the result being the confusion and chaos, distortion and deception we see today. Personal feelings and society's values dictate this fallen worldview.

For most of us, however, identity issues have more to do with a lack of confidence and security related to our physical characteristics and abilities, which affect our sense of well-being and self-esteem. I remember those teenage years when I felt awkward and unsure. I felt uneasy in relating to others, uncertain about my abilities. My brother and sister were the performers in our family and enjoyed putting on the entertainment. In my parents' home, we would put on skits, sing and entertain on our veranda. Can you guess what my role was? I used to stand hidden from view and pull the curtains open and closed, too shy to stand up in public. My natural choice of seat in church would be the back row. God slowly filled me with confidence as He prepared me to lead from the front.

All of us have been created with different temperament types. In his book *Spirit-Filled Temperament*, Tim La Haye explains four personality types as a way of understanding how we are fearfully and wonderfully made. These types were first described by Hippocrates but LaHaye gives them new significance. The purpose of the model is to help us better understand ourselves and others while being careful not to stereotype, compartmentalize, limit, or make superficial judgments. God has created us just the way we are. His intention is to draw out the best and refine the worst so that we may grow up into the people He intends. Lahaye also recognizes that each temperament has strengths and weaknesses.

These are my descriptions of the four temperament types:

Sanguine is the person who is the fun-loving, outgoing, bubbly, life of the party. The danger for this type is being limited to superficial froth with little substance.

Choleric is the go-getter who is driven to succeed, accomplish, and achieve. Their danger is overlooking, hurting or even stepping on people in the process of accomplishing that ambition.

Melancholic is the moody, pensive, creative person whose danger is potentially being ruled by self-absorbed erratic emotions.

Phlegmatic is the reflective, analytical and deliberate type who prefers to observe before jumping in and getting involved; this type can suffer from analysis paralysis.

It can be an interesting exercise to determine our temperament type. However, it is important to follow through with the next step to get the most out of the exercise, allowing the Holy Spirit to enrich the strengths of our natural temperament and refine the weaknesses in order to establish our true identity in Jesus Christ. This is the incredible gift He offers us.

I have recognized that I'm phlegmatic in being both reserved and analytical. God has used this aspect of my temperament to make me self-aware and reflective, as well as in being sensitive to others. However, He would not let me escape to seclusion or isolation, instead stretching and enabling me to build quality relationships. At the same time, I have a choleric side, the part of myself that drives me to initiate, envision, engage and complete new tasks. I also have a strong competitive streak, and the sports field offers an opportunity to exercise this side of my nature. My phlegmatic side has protected me from stepping over people to get anywhere. God has used my choleric side in concert with the phlegmatic me to fulfill one of my main ministries, building churches, networks and ministries. To do this means building relationships with people. While I've never been a naturally gregarious person, I developed into a more outgoing type as I grew in the confidence that came with knowing my identity and purpose in Christ. There were times in my pre-Christian development when I felt a melancholy negativity, but this was not really who I was.

As we discover who God is and what He has done, we find our identity, purpose and confidence. But what is our part in our maturity?

MATURITY MEANS ADDITION

Addition means to increase and improve, expand and grow. In his second letter, the apostle Peter offers additions to our life that ensure our calling and success as disciples. He begins, "*Make every effort to add to your faith…*" (2 Peter 1:5).

We must start with faith because faith is the starting point for salvation. I remember the first time I heard the idea of being saved. I had an immediate aversion to what sounded like crackpot religious talk. I did not need saving; after all, I had not done anything wrong—in my own eyes anyhow. Growing and adding to our life starts with recognizing that God expects perfection, and that we fall short of that standard. That means you, me, all of us, "*For all have sinned and fall short of the glory of God*" (Romans 3:23). Faith requires putting our complete trust in Jesus Christ who died in our place so that we might be freed from sin and be reconciled to God.

Faith also means we live our lives trusting in His provision and direction. One of the most majestic views in Canada is that of Niagara Falls. If I asked whether you believed I could walk a tightrope across the falls, what would you say? You would be right to be skeptical. But if my name was Nick Wallenda, a man who has accomplished this amazing feat, you would be right to say yes. However, if Nick asked you to jump on his back to carry you across, your belief might be seriously tested. This is the kind of faith that Jesus is looking for from us. Nick Wallenda has faith in Jesus as his Saviour and Lord, praying continually as he does this death-defying walk. Nick models for us how to pray through challenges, not focusing on the danger but constantly praising Jesus. Many people believe Jesus existed, was a good man, and so on, but the real test of faith is to believe that He gave His life for us, and that He is our salvation. He offers us everything by His grace, and we receive it by faith. The catch is that He expects us to give our lives over to Him.

As we live in this full-on relationship with the Lord Jesus Christ, we discover a new reality. God speaks to us through His living Word and His truth supersedes our understanding. A word is a thought communicated through language. God communicates His thoughts, desires, and will to us through His Word as recorded in the Bible. As we get to know God in this radical way, we see spiritual and eternal matters impacting the natural and temporal. Our prayer becomes: "*Your kingdom come, your will be done, on earth as it is in heaven*" (Matthew 6:10).

But Peter calls us to addition: "*Make every effort to add to your faith goodness*" (2 Peter 1:5). From our starting point of faith, we add qualities of God. Authentic goodness can only come from knowing the One who is good.

This real goodness depicts excellence expressed in deeds. It means aiming for the highest, being dissatisfied with second-best, doing all we can in every dimension of our lives. This includes being a good employee or employer, husband or wife, parent or friend. It involves all areas of ministry in the church, whether pastor, home group leader, dishwasher, Sunday school teacher, or whatever arena we are called to service.

Another essential arena of goodness can be seen in the moral choices we make. We live in a world where we are faced with many temptations. We have already seen God's way of dealing with moral choices and how the Bible introduces us to a very real evil power, Satan. The Fall in the Garden of Eden set the stage for our human predicament and struggle. We live with the consequences of a fallen human nature, a tendency towards evil. Through Jesus's death and resurrection, we have been saved, rescued from our history and given a new nature, one that provides the basis for goodness.

God never usurps our free will; we still have to make choices on a daily basis. Boundaries and directions are provided in Scripture and in nature for our guidance. As we obey them, God's blessings follow. As we disobey, we discover the consequences. It makes me think of how every year skiers, for the lure of pure untouched snow, go into out-of-bounds territory. There are signs and warnings. Yet these individuals don't believe the warnings apply to them, nor do they seem concerned they put the lives of brave first responders at risk when they have to be rescued. For some, the choice is fatal.

Similarly, the Ten Commandments are recognized by most civilized societies as a solid base for moral goodness. Yet there are those who think they know better, that the warnings don't apply to them. As they face the consequences of their actions, to quote the nursery rhyme, they try to find ways to put Humpty Dumpty together again, seeking human solutions to the human-caused destruction of a society torn apart by the consequences of adultery, murder, theft and greed. In effect, what the Bible regards as unacceptable becomes inverted so that good is regarded as evil, and evil is espoused as good. We desperately need to rediscover God's goodness for our own sake.

Peter's list of additions doesn't stop at goodness. He says, "*To goodness [add] knowledge*" (2 Peter 1:5). There are different kinds of knowledge ranging from education and book learning to street smarts and on-the-job training. True knowledge comes from knowing the One who knows all things. The more we know, the more we realize how little we know. Knowledge should bring humility, although in some cases, knowledge puffs up and leads to pride (1 Corinthians 8:1). Pride comes from being insecure, needing to use our knowledge to impress others and ourselves with a sense of self-importance. When Christians become proud and don't humble ourselves, often the Lord gives us a hand. We trip and fall; He prunes and disciplines us.

Knowledge gives us the power to get things done. My lack of mechanical knowledge frustrates my ability to fix my car when something goes wrong. My technical ignorance on the computer means that I need the help of my computer-savvy children more times than I would like to admit. Yet my knowledge of God and His Word has kept me on His path all these years. Knowing Him is the key to self-knowledge and fulfillment. It is another starting point to finishing well.

Peter continues, "*To knowledge, [add] self-control*" (2 Peter 1:6). Knowledge can be abused. We see this in the lessons Jesus teaches in a parable about a manager where He concludes, "*Whoever can be trusted with very little can also be trusted with much, and whoever is dishonest with very little will also be dishonest with much*" (Luke 16:10). We learn that the way we make decisions about small things affects the way we make larger decisions. But there is more. If we can't control our desires concerning earthly wealth and resources, Jesus asks, how can we be trusted with real power managing God's resources? *"So if you have not been trustworthy in handling worldly wealth, who will trust you with true riches? And if you have not been trustworthy with someone else's property, who will give you property of your own?"* (Luke 16:11-12) In case we interpret this parable as telling us to make worldly wealth our focus, Jesus gives this warning: *"No one can serve two masters. Either you will hate the one and love the other, or you will be devoted to the one and despise the other. You cannot serve both God and money"* (Luke 16:13).

From corporate entitlement to trade union tyranny to personal obsession with possessions, greed is a primary cause of spiritual deprivation. As we get to know the One who is both knowing and good, His desires become our desires. This is an area where God does much pruning, sometimes by giving us enough of our desires that we become sick of them, or at other times making us wait until we recognize the bankruptcy of our lust. Self-control goes hand in hand with taking responsibility for our actions but those lacking self-control usually blame everyone but themselves for the consequences of their choices.

"To self-control, [add] perseverance" (2 Peter 1:6). To bear fruit means we *"remain in [Christ]"* (John 15:5). To remain requires perseverance, persistence, endurance, steadfastness, devotion and commitment through to completion. It is important to be faithful, loyal and committed in the small things, so God can trust us with the larger things. I remember taking piano lessons, but I gave up after six months. Consequently, I can't play the piano. I regret that I didn't persevere. On the other hand, on the sports field or court, I have learned it is never over until it's over and will play to win until the last second. Too many of us expect instant gratification and give up when we face challenges. Jesus' parable of the sower (Luke 8) describes different conditions of the heart—hardness, faintness, shallowness—which make people give up on following Him. *"But the seed on the good soil stands for those with a noble and good heart, who hear the word, retain it, and by persevering produce a crop"* (Luke 8:15). God expects us to persevere and thus produce fruit.

I understand that there are many complex reasons for divorce, poor church attendance, broken relationships and absentee parents, but these can also be examples of having a faint heart. While there are times to leave and move on, we need to be willing to dig deep, overcome difficulties, become problem solvers, stay the course, and complete the task for which we have been commissioned. God often places us in situations as a test to find out what we are made of. Can you think of situations when you gave up when you should have persevered, or when you have remained in spite of difficulties? Perseverance is more than gritting one's teeth and never giving up; it includes facing our weakness and drawing on God for strength and power.

"*To perseverance, [add] godliness*" (2 Peter 1:6). Have you noticed how we become like the people we hang out and spend time with? Some even say owners and their pets start to look alike. Likewise, the more we spend time with God, the more we become like Him and begin to reflect His nature. As we participate in His divine nature, we escape the corruption in the world and take on His characteristics. Godliness means aligning ourselves in heart, mind and spirit, in our choices, values and ways—with Him. As the branch needs to remain attached to the vine to allow the life-giving sap to flow, so must we remain in Him, so that His life-giving Spirit flows through us and keeps us godly. As Christians, we who are Christ's and who are one with Him are called to be Christlike, as we "*are being transformed into His image with ever-increasing glory*" (2 Corinthians 3:18). Now there is a great addition!

"*To godliness, [add] mutual affection*" (2 Peter 1:7). As we begin to see God and reflect His character, we begin to see others differently. As our nature becomes more like His, we seek the best for others. Insecurity and low self-esteem bring out jealousy, envy, criticism and a desire to see others fail. When we know who we are, we are not threatened by others; we are happy to see them succeed. There is a story that explains that crabs can't get out of a bucket because as soon as one starts to climb up, the others drag him back down. Sadly, some people do this, trying to cut others down to their level of incompetence. Instead, we should be willing for others to stand on our shoulders if it will help them get a lift. By offering mutual affection, kindness and support, we all do better.

This leads to the next and final addition, a word so widely used and yet so little understood. "*And to mutual affection, [add] love*" (2 Peter 1:7). Maturity has to include love. But this demands another chapter. Love is mentioned so many times in the Bible, we'll give a little more space to this enormous topic.

Questions

As you read through Psalm 139, how does this impact your perception of God? Can you describe how you have known His omnipresence, omniscience, and omnipotence.

What is your primary temperament type? Number the types one through four according to how much each describes you. What are your strengths and weaknesses? Can you see how God is working in you through them? Are you making the most of the hand you have been dealt and the resources the Holy Spirit provides?

Jesus said, *"I have come that they may have life, and have it to the full"* (John 10:10). Share how your daily stresses and strains, relational conflicts, and unfulfilled expectations impact your ability to receive the promise of full life.

Looking back, think about what has been added to or subtracted from your life? List examples of how you have persevered or given up?

Describe one person in whom you see godliness. What stands out in this person's character?

What best describes your primary life experience—the crab-in-the-bucket syndrome or standing on someone's shoulders?

CHAPTER 6

All You Need is Love

The Beatles sang some fifty years ago that all we really needed was love. We are made with a built-in need to love and be loved. Love is the subject of songs, poems and sermons. The Bible has a lot to say about love. Jesus was not content to just talk about love; He embodied it.

Our English language's one word "love" is limited. The Greek language does better with three words amplifying and filling out the term:

Eros or self-gratifying love describes our basic need to love and be loved, and to reflect and receive significance, affirmation and acceptance. This includes erotic or sexual intimacy, which God intends to be fulfilled within the protection and cover of marriage as two become one.

Philia or friendship love includes all the qualities expressed in the well-known passage, 1 Corinthians 13.

Agape or self-sacrificial love can be seen in these words of Jesus: "*Greater love has no one than this: to lay down one's life for one's friends*" (John 15:13). This is the love exemplified and personified by Jesus. But what this looks like in our daily lives is sustained sacrifice, commitment and devotion. I heard someone say he was willing to lay down his life for Christ, only to turn down a request for help that meant he would be inconvenienced. If we can't put ourselves out in the small things, it is unlikely we will sacrifice in the big moments.

All three kinds of love are important, but where do we start to grow in love? Most start with their feelings, thoughts and opinions. However, once again Genesis 1:1 is the best place to start.

GOD LOVES US

God is love, we say. How does He communicate His love for us? You likely know this verse that gives us the answer: John 3:16. God loves us and gives us His first and best, expecting love, belief and obedience in return. Jesus challenges us to remain in this love: "*If you keep my commands, you will remain in my love...so that my joy may be in you and your joy may be complete. My command is this: Love each other as I have loved you*" (John 15:10-12).

The author Gary Chapman has written an excellent book on love languages (*Five Love Languages*), which shows ways we can give and receive love according to our temperament. Borrowing his concepts but supplying my own headings, I offer the five love languages, first applied to our relationship with God.

Affirmation: Where so much of life is about performance and conditional acceptance, God lovingly accepts us exactly where we are without reservation. "*While we were still sinners, Christ died for us*" (Romans 5:8). He affirms us for who we are. After all, He is our Creator.

Psalm 139 shows David's understanding of God's intimate affirmation. We respond to that affirmation by praising, believing and obeying Him.

Attention: God is interested in every aspect of our lives, from the top of our heads to what is going on inside them (Matthew 10:30). I remember someone seeking to know more of God finding this concept very difficult to grasp. They asked, "How can God, with all His responsibilities, be interested in the trivialities of my life?" The psalmist's answer is drawn from his personal experience. "*You know when I sit and when I rise; You perceive my thoughts from afar. You discern my going out and my lying down; You are familiar with all my ways.*" (Psalm 139: 2-3).

We can authentically respond by offering Him our devotion during the quiet time God longs to spend with each of us. Jesus stands at the door of our lives, but we still have to open it and give our attention to our attentive Father.

Appreciation: Many people have an image of God as a Scrooge-like figure for whom we have to perform and beg to get anything. In fact, He is a generous Father, "*who has blessed us in the heavenly realms with every spiritual blessing in Christ*" (Ephesians 1:3). As we receive the gift of His Son, we receive these blessings. In return we give Him our love, worship, time, energy, money and service. Tithing, giving Him the first-fruits of our labour, acknowledges that God is the One who has given us everything from the air we breathe to the land we cultivate and our ability to create wealth.

Action: Remember (from Chapter 1) that mistaken impression of God as a Creator who set the universe in motion and then sits back as it run its course? The book of Acts shows the activity of God working by the acts of the Holy Spirit through the early church. From Genesis to Revelation, we see a God who is actively involved with His Creation. God is active in the world, both sovereignly through His Holy Spirit and also in the activities of His people. Our only appropriate response is to actively serve Him and one another. This requires breaking out of our passivity, inertia, indifference and inaction.

Affection: God's very nature is love, and He has shown His love for us in a multitude of ways. But we are His Body; the physical expression of His love in and through us. We are His hands, His feet and His voice as we reach out and touch the lives of those around us. When we love Him with all our heart, soul, strength and mind, we will love one another.

LOVE ONE ANOTHER

As God has loved us, so are we to love one another. *"A new command I give you: Love one another. As I have loved you, so you must love one another. By this everyone will know that you are my disciples, if you love one another"* (John 13:34,35).

The five love languages teach us ways we can communicate this love. Chapman originally developed the languages for married partners, but the languages can be applied to all relationships. We all express and communicate love in different ways. God wants us to grow so we can meet the needs of those we love instead of loving in order to meet our own needs. Let's look and see which of these is our own primary way of communicating love in our human relationships.

Affirmation: Words are very powerful and can be used to build up or tear down. All of us need verbal affirmation—words from the heart which compliment, encourage and affirm us. There is the well-worn joke about the wife who asked her husband why he never said he loved her. He answered, "When we were married twenty-five years ago, I told you I loved you. If anything changes, I'll let you know." Sadly, there are many people who are not too different from this man, and they and their spouses are much the poorer for it.

Attention: This means giving quality time, as opposed to being an absentee, physically present but without the emotional focus which makes the other person feel special. I remember when my children were young and I was pushing them on a swing with one hand while holding a newspaper in the other. "Both hands, Daddy, both hands," they shouted at me. They were really telling me to give them my full, undivided and focused attention instead of reading the newspaper when I was supposed to be playing with them. How many people relate to their families with the newspaper or cellphone in one hand, and TV remote in the other?

Appreciation: Some people love to buy gifts, write notes or find some tangible way to express their appreciation. This can be a delightful expression of love. This is not the same as trying to buy love or compensating for a lack of attention with expensive gifts. A special treat is a great way of communicating love and creating memories. Many women would say it is still very important after many years. (I found out how important this is one year when I forgot my wife's birthday.) Giving and receiving gifts expresses the love language of appreciation.

Action: For some people, doing acts of service is the way they show love. This is one of those overlooked love languages in marriages. A wife may crave her husband's verbal affirmation without recognizing that he expresses his love in multiple ways by all the acts of kindness he offers her. In the same way some dads just love to do things with and for their children. They include them in their work, fix their bikes and make things for them. I am not very practical but I try. I remember the children coming to me with two planks of wood and asking me to make an airplane, a doll's house, or something complicated. In their mind was the one they saw at the toy store, and my best efforts were always a letdown; yet they deeply appreciated the effort.

The parable of the Good Samaritan is an example of loving by sacrificial effort. Jesus challenged His closest disciples with this story when He asked them who they thought acted as a neighbour to the man who was attacked by robbers. The best neighbour in the story was a despised Samaritan. Whether the one in need is the victim of a robbery, one who is emotionally deprived, the hurting person up the street, a stranger in church, or the drug addict asleep in the park, the question is the same: how are we acting as a good neighbour to them?

Affection: This is the language of physical touch, expressing love with hugs, kisses and holding hands. Being able to express affection in a natural and uninhibited way gives children a sense of real security and love.

Sadly, in today's world, sexual abuse has tarnished such physical expression. Children are taught at an early age about inappropriate touching, and this is necessary as a precautionary measure, but we can run the risk of losing the benefits of a truly good hug. When they were young, my children loved to climb up on my lap where they would sit and chat with me. The warmth and security of those fleeting moments before they got to be too grown up for that sort of thing provided them a sense of security and confidence. Today I enjoy that same kind of opportunity with my grandchildren. I would add a caution that physical expression should be primarily for those with whom there is relationship and permission. I have seen people appropriately cringe when someone they hardly know gets too close or touches them.

Each of these languages are important, and we need to grow in all of them. However, there are usually one or two which are the most natural ways we tend to express ourselves. Knowing our preferred love languages can help overcome misunderstanding. We need to be sensitive to which language really meets the needs of our spouse, children and others around us, and to try to communicate according to their needs.

Which is your predominant love language? Which is the one in which you would like love expressed to you? Are you willing to stretch to employ another language that is more natural to someone needing your love? Whether we are old or young, surrounded by people or in lonely isolation, here is a simple exercise that will transform our lives: find one person to show love this week.

We need to give and receive love. We can't exist in isolation. Some find love in marriage, while others are called to singleness or find themselves single due to circumstance or by choice. But whatever our situation, all of us need to give and receive the love of another.

Growing in maturity means growing in love. As we age, how we have loved in the past and how we are doing with our present relationships makes a huge difference in the quality of our lives. Elderly people can end up isolated, perhaps because of circumstances or because they never took the trouble to build quality relationships earlier in life. Others find it easier to slip into seclusion rather than put up with the inconvenience of having others around to disturb their superficial peace. True peace is not absence of noise nor of the people making that noise. The fruit of isolation is a social disease called loneliness.

ONLY THE LONELY

Roy Orbison famously sang about the heartbreak of lost love in the song "Only the Lonely." For many, broken relationships or not finding their one true love can lead to loneliness. But relationship of any kind is part of who we are and what we need to be fully human. With all our ingenuity and expertise, surely loneliness should not be a problem.

In our modern era, we have a new solution to isolation in social networking. How many of us tweet, text and use Facebook? This is the socializing of the present age, but with a catch: while it may feel like we have hundreds of friends on Facebook, it does not always satisfy our deepest need for relationship, to love and be loved. We can be very active in cyberspace, and yet be desperately lonely for real personal relationship.

How does it feel to be lonely? Have we ever gone into a new situation where we don't know anyone, or where we feel different? For some, that feeling never leaves. Have we had this longing for contact with someone—the sound of a voice, a touch perhaps? I can only begin to imagine what it must be like for those who have formerly shared a life with someone but now come back to an empty and silent apartment.

The cure for loneliness is relating to someone, both to people and to God. But often that's where the problem starts. To quote Charlie Brown, "I love mankind ... it's people I can't stand!" But, as much as we may find people frustrating, we really can't live completely alone. In his poem "Meditation XVII", John Donne wrote:

> No man is an island entire of itself; every man
> is a piece of the continent, a part of the main;
> if a clod be washed away by the sea, Europe is the less,
> as well as if a promontory were,
> as well as any manner of thy friends or of thine
> own were; any man's death diminishes me,
> because I am involved in mankind.
> And therefore never send to know for whom
> the bell tolls; it tolls for thee.[3]

God never intended for us to be islands on our own; on the contrary, He designed us for personal intimacy. The very word we use to describe our individual selves—person—is rooted in the concept of personally sharing ourselves.

God has created a way for us to be in relationship. We are His body, His people, His nation, His church. It is as we learn to cope with others in their annoying habits, irritating idiosyncrasies (and they with ours) that we grow and mature. This is one of God's primary ways to refine us. The process takes learning, humility and adjustment. While it may seem easier to retreat into perfect bubbles of me and mine, this is not God's purpose and therefore ultimately unworkable.

---

[3] Donne, John. "Meditation XVII" in Devotions Upon Emergent Occasions, and several steps in my Sickness, 1623.

Many live isolated in their little city boxes, surrounded by the masses, but having very little real relationship. In moments of honesty, they admit to being lonely. How can we be proactive to initiate real relationships? How can we bring people into our lives? Here are some starting points:

- Focus on someone else. Ask questions. Reach out. Connect. Share.
- Follow your interests. Be a joiner e.g. interest groups, sports clubs, community centres join activities and get to know people. Even chat to your plants, pet, self, TV.
- Keep in contact with family, friends, children, siblings, cousins, extended family. It takes work to phone, invite, or visit.
- Be part of the Body. Church is a place to meet people struggling to become whole persons just like you. God's plan is that we are part of His Body.
- Watch your attitude. Our attitude can attract or repel others. Wallowing in self-absorbed self-pity repels. Showing a genuine interest in others attracts.

In her poem "Solitude," Ella Wheeler Wilcox sums it up like this:

> Laugh, and the world laughs with you;
> Weep, and you weep alone…
> Rejoice, and men will seek you;
> Grieve, and they turn and go.
> They want full measure of all your pleasure,
> But they do not need your woe.
> Be glad, and your friends are many;
> Be sad, and you lose them all.[4]

These are virtues that produce well-rounded, fruitful, productive, mature persons living correspondingly genuine, loving human lives. The question for each of us to face is whether we are investing in our lives here and now so that that we produce this kind of fruit in the future. The reality is our personality and demeanour are the result of a combination of many influences, from our genetic makeup to the way we were brought up, and the wide variety of experiences, good and bad, we go through. It is what we do with them that can determine how we will behave, especially as we age.

When our defenses are down and our mental faculties diminish, our real selves can emerge. For some, this means becoming a cantankerous, miserable

[4] Wheeler Wilcox, Ella. 'Solitude' in The New York Sun (New York, 1883).

old codger; others reveal a sweet-tempered and genuinely beautiful spirit. What makes the difference? While behavioural and cognitive symptoms vary from person to person, what has been invested in our early years will return in some form later. The psalmist puts it best:

> *Blessed is the one who does not walk in step with the wicked or stand in the way that sinners take or sit in the company of mockers, but whose delight is in the law of the Lord, and who meditates on his law day and night. That person is like a tree planted by streams of water, which yields its fruit in season and whose leaf does not wither—whatever they do prospers.* (Psalm 1:1-3)

Once again, where we start determines how and where we finish, and this impacts the quality of our lives.

Let me tell you about my parents. As children, my brother, sister and I knew our mother as a strict disciplinarian and task master who expected much from us. She also pushed us to achieve, encouraging us to study, play sport and travel. When we grew up, my father would have been happy if we had all built houses in the same neighbourhood and stayed close together. While there were times in our lives when we lived in the same city, we also scattered to different parts of the globe for studies, work and opportunities. Both my parents were strong churchgoers, but went to different churches, my father to the Congregational Church where his family had been stalwart supporters for years, and my mother following her upbringing went to the Anglican Church. It was one of the differences between my parents. However, we knew they loved us, felt secure in our family and home, and had a happy childhood. Both of my parents came to commit their lives to Jesus as Saviour and Lord.

My mother had a reserved temperament which combined with strong opinions to make her seem formidable, aloof and even unfriendly to some. She was also very accomplished, competent and respected in her administrative work. In her seventies, she contracted Alzheimer's disease. This disease affects many people as they age, all differently. It is a real challenge for families to know how to cope. For us, this was where things got interesting. The more the Alzheimer's took hold, the less my mother could remember and the more incoherent she became. At the same time, she became sweeter, kinder and more loving as well. In the care home where she eventually lived, she was extremely popular and was well-loved by staff and patients alike. Going to the dining room, she would gracefully walk around to the tables, greeting and chatting to everyone as though she was the hostess or the queen. We used to have long telephone conversations that didn't make much sense, yet they meant so much to her and to me. I appreciated every precious call as I knew that one day the phone would fall silent. When she died at ninety years old, she did so as she lived, with a peaceful grace and dignity.

As we delight in the presence and the Word of the Lord, so this delight will impact and shine from our inner spirit. God promises that we "*are being transformed into His image with ever increasing glory*" (2 Corinthians 3:18). If we have a relationship with Him, we will never be alone. If we know God our Father, we are brought into His family as His sons and daughters. As we belong to God, we belong to and have fellowship with one another. Therefore we never need be lonely. As we know Him and His love, we know we are loved and can love others.

One of the most meaningful ways to meet our basic needs for relationship, to love and be loved, is through the gift of marriage. It is not only the most intimate of human relationships; it is also the model of Christ's relationship with His Church (Revelation 21:2). This is why "*The Lord God said, "It is not good for the man to be alone. I will make a helper suitable for him"* (Genesis 2:18).

Questions

List some of the ways you have experienced God's love.

Which of the love languages best expresses your relationship with your Heavenly Father? Why are these your favourites?

Describe your predominant love language in terms of how you communicate love. Now describe the one in which you would like love expressed to you.

Read John 13:34,35. How do you respond to the criticism of the church: if this is how we are meant to demonstrate that we are disciples, why is it that Christians find it so hard to get along with one another?

Read 1 Corinthians 13: 4-8a. Together with the previous John passage, describe how you have experienced this kind of love in the Church.

If you are not yet part of a small/growth/home group, think about getting involved with one.

CHAPTER 7
One Plus One Equals One

Few would object to the idea that family is the foundation of our culture, or that marriages and families are in serious trouble in our time. Many children are being raised without the God-given protection of two parents, a man and a woman. One in two marriages ends in divorce. At the same time, with so many additional social problems connected to marriage and family, we must acknowledge something is fundamentally out of alignment. If we are more interested in solving our problems than defending our positions, we must look at what Scripture has to say about our problems. We will look at this in two parts: God's intention; and, caring for one another when we mess up. (If anything I say offends, please hear me out before closing the book.)

Before we get to how marriage is meant to work, we have to understand the foundations of marriage. Ephesians offers the big picture. We start with God's purpose for all His Creation, *"to bring unity to all things in heaven and on earth under Christ"* (Ephesians 1:10). The same principle applies to marriage, which reflects the intimacy of God's relationship with His Church.

In math, one plus one equals two, but in marriage, one plus one makes one. Paul builds his argument on this from Genesis 2:24: *"'For this reason a man will leave his father and mother and be united to his wife, and the two will become one flesh.' This is a profound mystery—but I am talking about Christ and the church"*

(Ephesians 5:31,32). In true biblical style, this simple statement contains layers of meaning. Growing into adulthood, couples leave the source of their nurturing and protection—their parents—to create their own relationship. Becoming one includes the intimacy of physical sexual union and much more as two lives become intertwined at every level from emotional and spiritual to economic and social. At the heart of oneness, qualities such as trust and faithfulness are sealed in the marriage vow or covenant.

This is God's plan, His gift to us for our well-being. It is so important that Paul describes it as a visual representation of the relationship between Christ and His Church. Jesus is head over all things, as demonstrated in unity and oneness in Creation, in the Church, and in marriage. This is the exact same principle Jesus expressed in an encounter with religious leaders.

IS IT LAWFUL?

One day, a group of Pharisees asked Jesus whether it was lawful for a couple to divorce. Interestingly, the Pharisees start from a legalistic point of view: is it lawful? At the time, there were two schools of thought on marriage among the Pharisees: the Shammai were more strict and only allowed divorce for a significant reason, while the Hillel were more liberal and allowed divorce for every reason no matter how trivial. This was the basis for Moses's certificate of divorce, to protect the women from hardness of heart. Today we still have that divide, and divorce statistics in the church are often not better than in the rest of society.

Jesus does not answer the Pharisees directly, but instead quotes Genesis (Mark 10: 6-8). Jesus corrects and redirects the focus to where it should be: the nature of marriage. This is His declaration of intent, calling marriage a lifelong monogamous union between a man and woman. The Pharisees want to find a reason that justifies divorce—is it lawful, is it permissible?—but Jesus cares only about the heart of the matter.

We can add all sorts of today's questions about what is lawful and permissible. If we do away with this core verse, we can redefine and re-engineer and make up any belief or value system we want. It all depends on our starting point. God gives His truth through the revelation of His Word. We can accept and obey, or not. But the inescapable reality is that when we ignore or disobey and make up our own subjective interpretation of truth, we deify ourselves. While many in our society are deceived by the cultural shift, God calls us to stand up for His standards. We see the result of a world out of harmony with its Creator, in a total mess and scrambling to find solutions. Spearheaded by the gods of Hollywood, we see people deciding to live together without commitment, ridicule virginity and abstinence until marriage, and redefine marriage to include same-sex relationships.

A recent survey in the US found thirty-nine percent of people believe marriage is obsolete. One in three young people grow up in fatherless homes; studies show these children are much more likely to do poorly in school, commit crimes, and live in poverty and dysfunctional relationships themselves, perpetuating and spreading their unhappiness. The social consequences are directly related to the relational roots. Children who grow up not having a loving family to nurture, teach or care for them miss out having godly role models of husband and wife, mother and father. They are raised not knowing the truth of absolutes, boundaries and self-control, or the values of loyalty, faithfulness and commitment. The dysfunctional status quo persists until someone wakes up and realizes that, for the best results, we need to follow the instructions of the Maker.

SEX AND THE CITY (OR ANYWHERE ELSE)

God has set the limits of sexual activity to be found within the commitment of a secure and loving relationship between a man and a woman: marriage. When the marriage vow is broken, like any sin, there is a ripple effect, leaving a trail of broken people. Jesus closes His argument with the words we use at the wedding ceremony, "*Therefore what God has joined together, let no one separate*" (Mark 10:9). God takes marriage so seriously that He personally takes the responsibility for joining husband and wife as one. Individuals are not meant to decide to un-join, mess with, tear apart, separate or divorce what God has blessed in union. God makes His will very clear, saying He hates divorce (Malachi 2:16). Remarriage after divorce, except in the case of unfaithfulness, is even considered adultery. Jesus says, "*Anyone who divorces his wife and marries another woman commits adultery*" (Mark 10:11, 12).

Paul cites the spiritual consequence of adultery in terms of promiscuity: "*Do you not know that he who unites himself with a prostitute is one with her in body... The two become one flesh*" (1 Corinthians 6:16). Paul makes no distinction between promiscuity and having any partner outside the marriage bond elsewhere in his letter. If we only see through the eyes of the physical, extra-marital sex seems to offer variety and pleasure, even if it is fleeting. Through spiritual eyes, however, we see that this results in a sort of emotional and spiritual fragmentation as we split part of ourselves off at each sexual encounter. It is impossible to unscramble scrambled eggs. In an age where multiple sexual encounters are not only regarded as normative, but glorified, is it any wonder we have a society of scrambled misfits.

IS IT BETTER TO REMAIN SINGLE?

You may be thinking, wow, all this sounds tough. For the disciples it sounded impossible, so much so that they wondered whether "*it is better not to marry*" (Matthew 19:10). Jesus answers by saying the some are called to singleness "*for the sake of the kingdom of heaven*" (Matthew 19:12). Singleness is a response to the call of God .

Paul recommended that everyone remain as they are whether married or single (1 Corinthians 7:8-9). The context was that he believed Christ was returning any moment. Because of the "*present crisis*" (1 Corinthians 7:26), his intent was we should not be distracted from full devotion to the Lord. Some teaching on singleness has been applied out of context, and I believe is seriously flawed. The Roman Catholic Church has a policy of celibacy for priests and nuns. This was introduced on and off over centuries. It was first suggested by a pope in 304 but was rejected by the Council of Nicea in 325. In 1139 celibacy was reintroduced by Pope Gregory V11, but only at the Council of Trent in 1563 was it officially reaffirmed. The decision not to marry was intended to allow a person to be set aside and devoted in holy service of the Lord. The accounts of terrible abuse by those in "holy orders" are a disgrace and a serious blot on the witness of the Church. Engaging in secret forbidden sinful behaviours after choosing celibacy makes no sense. Perhaps such people should read the next part of the passage: "*If his passions are too strong, and he feels he ought to marry, he should as he wants*" (1 Corinthians 7:36). There are those who are called to celibacy, but this should be in obedience to the Holy Spirit, not legislated as a human command. Paul draws that distinction: he acknowledges that celibacy is his recommendation but not necessarily the Lord's command. He knows marriage is normative for human beings.

THE JOY OF MARRIAGE

Whatever our situation, God has a gift, purpose and plan for each of us. Marriage, symbolizing the relationship between Christ and his Church, is a most dynamic dimension of that plan for most of us. Of course He offers that same oneness with Himself, whether we are married or single, and this oneness is the basis for all our relationships. No relationships are easy, but it is God who has joined people together; we are not alone. He is with us, helping us, because He wants to see us fulfill our lives as much as our vows, remaining joined till death us do part.

Marriages go through life stages just as individuals do. There is a season, especially in those early years, for sowing seeds. Once the initial glow wears off, the hard work begins. We adapt and learn to communicate, share and work together, offer grace and forgiveness for shortcomings, encourage and build each other up. There will be times when we feel let down, may be tempted to throw in the towel, and think the grass is greener with someone else. This is the time to show perseverance, commitment and honour to the vows we took before God.

Those vows are beautiful on the wedding day and they can ring true for the rest of our lives. There does come a time when the work pays off, and the seeds sown bear fruit. Sadly, some miss the best because they give up too soon, and don't persevere. The seeds of trust and honour, love and affection, commitment and service in all the ups and downs of life blossom into a level of comfortable companionship and deep fulfillment unequaled in human relationship. There is no need to impress or impose; we can simply enjoy being together. This is God's intention in the gift of lifelong monogamous marriage between a husband and wife. It is the hope of every wedding couple, and the blessing for those who enjoy God's best. There is nothing more beautiful than a married couple who are knit together in support, love and care for one another *till death us do part.*

IS DIVORCE THE UNFORGIVABLE SIN?

What happens when marriages fail? Is divorce the unforgivable sin? The reality is that because of our hard-hearted nature we do fail, including in marriage. We are all sinners who mess up all the time.

Jesus shuts the door on the easy divorce, but are there extenuating circumstances that allow divorce? Jesus does mention an exception. *"I tell you that anyone who divorces his wife, except for sexual immorality, and marries another woman commits adultery"* (Matthew 19:9). As we have seen, marriage is a union of two lives at every level. Adultery breaks that union, but there are more As which destroy marriages and families. Abuse, particularly physical but also emotional, is one. Addictions are another. Still another is Abandonment, when someone breaks the vow of commitment. These four As contravene the intent of marriage, and the consequence is destruction. When one is the victim of these behaviours, what should be done?

The starting point is asking what God wants. He wants marriage not divorce. He wants us to love our sinful partners as He loves us. He wants us to see our mate the way He does, as the person with whom we are joined as one. When our marriage is in trouble, one should seek counsel, healing and reconciliation. This can be painful, and will need all the qualities of grace and forgiveness of the Holy Spirit. Paul's instruction is: *"A wife must not separate from her husband. But if she does, she must remain unmarried or else be reconciled to her husband. And a husband must not divorce his wife"* (1 Corinthians 7:10, 11) . There are many examples of couples who share openly about their struggles and hardships yet choose to stay together.

How? Much more can be said, but I share one word that is largely misunderstood: submission. *"Submit to one another"* (Ephesians 5:21). Submission is not a popular word today because it is usually associated with subservience. But submission simply means I put someone else first, seeking what is best for them. And that is exactly what our marriage relationship should be about. However, because of our selfish sinful nature, it is hard, if not impossible. The second part of that verse is the key *"…out of reverence for Christ."* As we revere, submit, worship and serve Him, we learn to submit to one another, and love with self-sacrificial love.

You may ask what if there comes a time when someone contravenes all that marriage means, and all resources have been depleted? Can divorce be the lesser of two evils and the healthiest course of action for all concerned? Divorce is a last resort that should be taken only when all attempts at reconciliation have failed, and in consultation with mature spiritual counsel. For those who have been hurt by divorce, it is not the end of the world. There is life after divorce. The consequences are often extreme and leave people brokenhearted and crushed in their spirit. I have worked with people going through this process, and I know how painful it is.

Can we turn to God when we have let Him down, and perhaps feel let down by Him? We know that He is in the redemption business. He speaks directly to us through His Word: *"The Lord is close to the brokenhearted and saves those who are crushed in spirit"* (Psalm 34:18). He is working out His purpose in all of our lives, whatever the situation or immediate pain we experience.

God's part was accomplished on the Cross. Jesus took our sin onto Himself so we could be free to experience His love, forgiveness, healing and restoration. There is hope after divorce, as there is after any kind of failure. While the consequences may always be there—the disappointment, sadness and pain—we have a loving God who knows what we are going through, and provides the resources to help us. He gives us His Word, and He gives us the Holy Spirit. Instead of resorting to a lawyer with human limitations, the Holy Spirit is our Advocate (John 14:26). He is the Comforter and Counsellor who comes alongside us no matter what our situation to bring us His peace. He leads us into all truth and gives His wisdom as we struggle to make right choices. He enables us to offer forgiveness as we receive forgiveness. Psalm 51 is the prayer of a forgiven sinner, David the adulterer and murderer. *"Have mercy on me, O God...Wash away all my iniquity and cleanse me from m y sin...Create in me a pure heart, O God, and renew a steadfast spirit within me"* (Psalm 51:1,2, 10).

The challenge for all of us is, on the one hand, to uphold God's clearly stated will and intention for marriage. On the other hand, we balance this with compassion and grace for those who fail to live up to His will. We also need to offer restoration and recovery for all who have been affected in every way. It is my hope that we learn to do all three well.

How we relate to one another—especially our marriage partners, our children and their children—will impact the legacy we leave behind. What do we have to do now to invest in our legacy? That will be the question for the next chapter.

Questions

Do we approach moral issues from a viewpoint of law, feelings, rights or some other viewpoint?

Is divorce the unforgivable sin? How do we balance wedding vows with the four As mentioned as possible reasons to leave a marriage? How do we balance upholding God's law with pastoral care?

In our Christian circles, do single people—whether by choice or circumstance—feel included, accepted and respected? How can we be supportive?

What does the word submission mean to you? What difficulties do you find in *"submitting to one another"*?

How can we prevent marriages from declining into stalemate and keeping the joy alive till death us do part?

Reflective Prayer

God has a purpose for all of us in whatever stage and condition of life we find ourselves. Let us take this time to remember and pray for those who are:

Single—Lord we invite You to be our companion, to receive Your comfort in loneliness, Your guidance in our hopes, and entrust our future into Your care, knowing that You have a plan for our life.

Divorced—Lord, we invite You to heal the memories, the hurt, the past. Forgive us as we forgive those who have hurt us. We pray recovery and restoration for those impacted, especially children. Lord, be with those going through stresses and strains at this time.

Married—Lord, we give thanks for those whom You have given us as our husband/wife, and we receive Your grace, patience, and love. May our marriages reflect Your intentions and love. May our homes be a haven of peace and blessing.

Bereaved—Lord, we pray for those who have lost their lifelong husbands or wives. We remember and give thanks for them. We pray for those caring for their loved ones who are ailing and aging.

Children—Lord we pray for children who are growing up in an increasingly hostile world, as victims of all kinds of abuse and neglect, the tragedies of war, and families in crisis. Provide them Your loving comfort and security.

Parents—We remember fathers and mothers, that they may know Your strength, wisdom and love to serve their families.

CHAPTER 8

Investing in a Legacy

How do we prepare now for those later days when aging effects catch up with us? What will we be remembered for? What legacy will we leave behind? One of the most important keys to answering these questions is finding and knowing our purpose.

Consider a related question. What makes some families so strong in a certain field that they leave a legacy for generations? For example, the Trudeau name is well known in Canadian politics, as are the Kennedys and Bushes in the USA. Rockefeller is synonymous with finance, Ford with cars, and Gates or Jobs with computers. At the church where I pastored, we built on a legacy left by founding pioneers, Edward and Mary Cridge.

Some drift through life, existing from one day to the next without ever discovering the reason for their lives. Others seem very successful by all the usual standards yet come to the end of their lives full of regret. Even those who seem to have everything—fame, wealth, and success—often have a void they try to fill with a volatile mixture of drugs, alcohol and an unrestrained lifestyle, only to discover these lead to an early grave. We are even more puzzled by the rich and famous people who seem to have it all and yet commit suicide. If only they knew that there is a God who loves them and promises that every hair on every head is

. While mental illness can play a part, these tragedies all point to the
or a spiritual point to life.

WHAT IS THE POINT?

A great cloud of novelists, poets and songwriters lament about the angst and pointlessness of everything. Such a view is not new: "*I have seen all the things that are done under the sun; all of them are meaningless, a chasing after the wind*" (Ecclesiastes 1:14). Sadly, many engage in pursuits that in the end amount to vanity and meaninglessness, efforts that are as pointless as chasing the wind. Even more sad, they can't see it. The limitation is that these are things under the sun. But true meaning transcends earthly existence.

For some, the driving force of life is negative emotions, like a forty-year-old man's childhood memory of being out boating with his younger brother. The boat capsized and his brother drowned. The man could never shake feelings of responsibility and guilt. Other negative forces drive people—resentment, anger, fear, the need for approval. For many it is materialism, the drive to succeed or become wealthy. There are those who will go to any lengths (including unethical and even criminal activities) in their quest to satisfy their existential hungers. Once achieved, do they satisfy? Most would recognize the answer is no yet they continue to pursue a goal they know will let them down.

What does God have to say about our legacy? "*I, the Lord Your God, am a jealous God…showing love to a thousand generations of those who love me and keep my commandments*" (Exodus 20:5, 6). Building a legacy for God's Kingdom is different from a legacy of this world, because it is based on eternal values. It's all about our relationship with Him. We have already seen one of the main directives from Jesus—"*Remain in me, as I also remain in you. No branch can bear fruit by itself; it must remain in the vine. Neither can you bear fruit unless you remain in me*" (John 15:4).

Increasing our legacy often involves dealing with setbacks and rising above obstacles.

I have had two major instances of starting over in my life. Little did I imagine in the joy and sense of accomplishment that comes with ordination that eleven years later I would be resigning my post without knowing where I was going. It was painful and confusing. I felt my ministry, not to mention my legacy, was in tatters. God redeemed all this and we started a new ministry with a focus on Him. Just five years later, we uprooted our family and started from scratch in a new country on the other side of the world, in Victoria on Vancouver Island, British Columbia, Canada.

It becomes more difficult to be transplanted as we get older. I spent at least four years trying to get off Vancouver Island as it seemed like we were cut off from the rest of the world. On the surface there were cultural similarities between South Africa and Canada, but we also soon discovered differences, and struggled to adapt. We began to understand the secular national religion of hockey, tried snow skiing instead of surfing, and got used to gray drizzly days being described as lovely weather. Canadians are very polite, even passive, but disagreements bring out an aggressive side. For some, that means standing and fighting, but many took the line of least resistance as they simply cut and ran. I shouldn't complain as this exemplifies the same uneasy relationship we have with God.

We were formerly foreigners excluded from citizenship in His Kingdom. *"But now in Christ Jesus you who once were far away have been brought near by the blood of Christ... Consequently, you are no longer foreigners and strangers, but fellow citizens with God's people and also members of his household"* (Ephesians 2:13, 19).

I became a citizen of heaven when I met Jesus Christ and a citizen of Canada in 1997. For the latter I had to sit a test and affirm my allegiance to my new country. In both, I had to learn similar principles. I had to bloom where I was planted, be prepared to stay and commit to the new place, and develop devotion and discipline, perseverance and endurance in completing my assigned task. During times of uncertainty and upheaval, I found my strength and direction in the place where I spend time every day, the Word of God. Here we find flawed human characters called into service by the Lord, yet dealing with real challenges, needing to reboot and start over—just like us. The result is a legacy to remember, one that offers us encouragement and a model to emulate. One part of that legacy concerns a man who struggled with childlessness yet became the father of nations and a patriarch of our faith; the promises given to Abraham have become part of our heritage.

ABRAHAM — FATHER OF NATIONS

Abram was a successful farmer minding his own business in his hometown of Haran when God spoke to him, saying, *"Go from your country, your people, and your father's household to the land I will show you"* (Genesis 12:1). Abram was asked to give up everything that composed his identity—his country, his nationality, and his family—to go to a land God would show him. Leave and go is the essence of God's call. *"So Abram went, as the Lord had told him"* (Genesis 12:4).

Abram had a clear mandate from God not much different from our own. We learn how to respond and put into practice basic principles of discipleship beginning with what I call the "go" mandate. As we look back on our own personal journeys, we can see God at work, giving direction, overcoming obstacles, steadily moving us forward. Go means one step at a time beginning with the first one.

There will be disappointments that leave us feeling let down, changes which can bring uncertainty, and there will always ne unknowns. In the midst of these uncertainties, we are called to walk in faith. We wonder if we can really trust God. Because people let us down all the time, this can increase our cynicism about anyone, including God, keeping their word. Politicians and corporations often don't keep their promises, children discover that parents are fallible, and innocent new Christians are confused to discover fellow church folk are also flawed human beings. So why trust God? As we meet Abram embarking on his journey, we see him being transformed from a wandering pilgrim into a faithful patriarch. At the same time, we are introduced to characteristics of God that answer many of our questions. Let's look at Abram's journey and his transformation into Abraham, so we can apply the lessons to our own lives.

God chose Abram by grace, not because he had earned or deserved it, nor because he was young and limber. How many times in Genesis 17 do we read God saying I will? Count them as you read.

After declaring His identity to Moses—I AM —here God declares His will. He is the One who initiates, makes, gives, establishes, confirms and wills into reality. Abram and Sarai are given name changes to confirm this call and promise. Abram (exalted father) becomes Abraham (meaning "father of nations"). Sarai and Sarah both mean princess, but Sarah gives additional significance, meaning princess of many.

COVENANT

God has a way of confirming His promises that is summed up in the word covenant. As we face uncertainties and unknowns in setting out on a new faith journey, it is good to remind ourselves of the basis for our faith and trust.

At its most basic, a covenant is an agreement, promise or contract which can be interpreted as a will or testament. The Greek word used is *diatheke,* in which terms are offered by one party which the other can accept or reject. Literally, the word means to cut by the shedding of blood. In the Old Testament we learn that *"Life…is in the blood…it is the blood that makes atonement for one's life"* (Leviticus 17:11), *"and without the shedding of blood there is no forgiveness"* (Hebrews 9:22). The Old Covenant required the blood of animals, such as the lamb at Passover. It is Jesus's shed blood which activates the New Covenant: *"This is my blood of the covenant"* (Matthew 26:28). To confirm His Old Covenant, God gave Abram an outward sign as a reminder of what He offers: circumcision (Genesis 17:7, 11). The New Covenant sign is baptism; like shed blood baptism signifies activation by death inasmuch as the literal meaning of the Greek word for baptism refers to burial. We see these two outward signs being used to describe the same inward spiritual reality:

> *In Him you were also circumcised with a circumcision not performed by human hands. Your whole self ruled by the flesh was put off when you were circumcised by Christ, having been buried with Him in baptism, in which you were also raised with Him through your faith in the working of God, who raised Him from the dead.* (Colossians 2:11-12)

Baptism is a seal or sign of belonging. It says that my dues have been paid and I can now enter and participate in God's Kingdom business. Understanding and recalling this reality can make all the difference when we reach a point of desperation or at any time in the journey.

God declares His will and makes promises as part of this covenant. Abram is promised a new home and country and that his descendants would become a great nation. This covenant remains operational today, but who are the descendants for generations to come? These descendants are found in Israel whose possession of the promised land is rooted in God's covenant promise, and in those of us who are Christians.

Remember that a will describes the inheritance left to the heirs of a person who has died. In Christ we are heirs of Abraham. *"He redeemed us in order that the blessing given to Abraham might come to the Gentiles through Christ Jesus,...by faith we might receive the promise of the Spirit...If you belong to Christ, then you are Abraham's seed, and heirs"* (Galatians 3:14, 29). We are heirs of God's estate or Kingdom in Christ. The Old Covenant promises of a physical land point to a fulfillment in Christ and entrance into a heavenly promised land of which we are all heirs.

God invites and sets the terms of the covenant, offers benefits and promises, and expects us to respond. We can trust God, not because we deserve what He offers, but because He has made a promise to fulfill His covenant with His covenant people. That is all God's part, but it is dependent on us doing our part.

God says to Abram, *"As for you, you must keep my covenant, you and your descendants after you for the generations to come"* (Genesis 17:9).

God expects us to be blameless and perfect before Him. That is not easy, except that *"For it is by grace you have been saved, through faith—and this is not from yourselves, it is the gift of God"* (Ephesians 2:8, 9). God calls and gives by His grace. We respond by faith. This is how we receive salvation and God's promises. Faith is essential: *"Without faith it is impossible to please God"* (Hebrews 11:6).

What is faith? *"Now faith is confidence in what we hope for and assurance about what we do not see"* (Hebrews 11:1). Abram was told to leave all that gave him identity and to go to a new land. He did not know where he was going, yet he obeyed and went. Faith and obedience are interlinked. While our blamelessness is a gift of grace, we have to put one foot in front of the other as we put into practice what we have received. This means making right choices by obeying God's way. We take one step at a time in what becomes a journey of many steps.

Even though God's promise didn't make sense as Abraham and Sarah were past child-bearing age, they both trusted that God would fulfill His promise of having a child (Hebrews 11:11). Abraham's actual first response was to fall face down and laugh (Genesis 17:17). While that doesn't sound like a great faith response, yet in spite of his flawed faith, he is remembered as a man of faith. Don't you find that encouraging? Being rooted in a covenant relationship with the living God, we learn that walking by faith in the Spirit is more real than relying on our senses. Faith is seeing beyond the natural with the eyes of the supernatural, beyond the physical into the spiritual. In the big picture, when we are born of the Spirit, we become strangers in this world as our citizenship, our destiny and our reason for living become heaven-focused. As we are filled with the Holy Spirit who is our deposit or assurance of heaven, He aligns our heart with God's. Our longings become God's desires, our hopes become His intentions. We can be fully certain of those hopes. We can become certain of the things unseen by the senses, but seen in the Spirit, for we have learned to walk by faith and not by sight. In the Old and New Covenant, that call to leave and go is the same.

FOLLOW ME

Jesus's call to the disciples was very similar to the one given by God to Abram: to follow Him. He tells us to leave all that gives us identity and security, to come and follow Him, and He will make us into people who can serve Him and others, make you into an instrument and witness. All the talents He gave us—whether that is to be an accountant, sports player, electrician, chef, painter, musician and so on—can be used in the building of His Kingdom. We can take those caring, driving, thoughtful, reflective, creative traits He gave us and bring them to Him, letting Him re-create and make us into the people He intended us to be. Those gifts of administration, teaching, leadership, service, compassion, and so many more, are for ministry to bless others as He has blessed us.

Jesus invites us to come to Him, to follow Him. But He also calls us to leave something behind, as we turn around, and take a step of faith. Dietrich Bonhoeffer sums it up beautifully when he writes in *The Cost of Discipleship*, "The disciple simply burns his boats and goes ahead. He is called out...The old life is left behind, and completely surrendered. The disciple is dragged out of his relative security into a life of absolute insecurity...out of the realm of the finite that is in truth, into the absolute security and safety of the fellowship of Jesus... into the realm of infinite possibilities."

When we are approaching a new stage of our journey, there are lots of unknowns. But stepping out in faith is not the same as stepping into the dark. Under our feet is a covenant which provides more security than any earthly security ever could, and this enables us to be sure of what is unseen. In summary, God loved us so much that He gave us a deal, a covenant, which is signed in His blood to show His good faith, to enter into partnership with Him. He offers all the benefits and privileges of His Kingdom to us and gives us access to His estate. In return, He expects us to believe His Word, keep His covenant, and obey His commands as we walk by faith and as He makes us into His image. I believe that in whatever stage of life we find ourselves, God has a plan for our future, a plan to bless, to multiply and extend His Kingdom.

God expects us to see with the eyes of faith. Once again Abraham provides us some foundational principles, this time described by the prophet Isaiah.

LOOK BACK ON OUR HERITAGE

God tells us we are to look back to our roots, our heritage, history, family, spiritual beginnings. *"Look to the rock from which you were cut and to the quarry from which you were hewn; look to Abraham, your father, and to Sarah, who gave you birth. When I called him he was only one man, and I blessed him and made him many"* (Isaiah 51:1, 2).

At the time Isaiah wrote, Israel was in captivity while Jerusalem was a pile of rubble. Things seemed pretty hopeless. But into this scene, Isaiah brings an explicit word of encouragement, reminding the Israelites to look back and to remember Abraham and Sarah. Abraham and Sarah must have felt that same hopelessness, as they waited twenty-five years to see the fulfillment of God's promise of descendants. Even then it only started with one child, but the blessings came and the one became many.

We can look back to our own spiritual heritage. I have already shared my personal faith journey as part of my formation. The last twenty years of my pastoral career were spent at Church of Our Lord, Victoria, BC. The heritage of this church was built on the shoulders of its founding father, Edward Cridge, who started the church in 1874. He and his wife, Mary, pioneered many service activities in the city. Life in those days was not easy. The Cridges buried four of their nine children, who died of scarlet fever and black measles. But their spiritual family multiplied greatly as many have been blessed by the ministries they started. They rose above their own tragedy in caring for orphaned and abandoned children. This led to what is now known as The Cridge Centre for the Family, which today is a multimillion-dollar mission providing seniors housing, a children's preschool and daycare, a brain injury centre, women's shelter, and affordable housing, to name a few services. The Cridges cared for the sick, leading to the start of the Royal Jubilee Hospital. They didn't try to leave a legacy. They simply served the needs of the community, and a legacy grew. At the same time a DNA of mission was firmly established at Church of Our Lord.

Look back on your journey. Look back to the quarry, the rock from which we were cut. There may be times when we think our life looks like a heap of rubble as we survey the destruction around us. We have all been there. Whatever our situation, God speaks directly to it:

> *The LORD will surely comfort Zion and will look with compassion on all her ruins; he will make her deserts like Eden, her wastelands like the garden of the LORD. Joy and gladness will be found in her, thanksgiving and the sound of singing.* (Isaiah 51:3)

We can look back to a time when we knew the blessing of the Lord, perhaps the moment we came to know Him. We look back to the rock from which we were cut. God is in the redemption business. He can clean up our messes and turn the wasteland of our lives into a garden.

MISSION MANDATE

Jesus took His own mandate from Isaiah 61, declaring it in the synagogue in Nazareth. We cannot do better than follow Him.

The Spirit of the Lord is on me, because He has anointed me to proclaim good news to the poor. He has sent me to proclaim freedom for the prisoners and recovery of sight for the blind, to set the oppressed free, to proclaim the year of the Lord's favor. (Luke 4:18)

This mission statement combines three primary threads for me: the opening is charismatic or Pentecostal language; the proclamation of good news is the focus of evangelicals (evangel means message, which is the Gospel we are called to proclaim); finally, the social gospel with its emphasis on care for the poor and oppressed is a touchstone for another whole wing of the church. I don't believe it is a coincidence that all three are intertwined. This passage has been my own mission mandate for years, both in South Africa and in Canada.

As I reflect on my twenty years at Church of Our Lord (affectionately known as COOL), it has been an incredible journey. We began with a vision to restore the exterior of the church. Built in 1876 in Carpenter Gothic design, it was pretty run down. On the street I heard someone say, "Isn't it a pity they don't look after that beautiful old church." I asked the leaders to pretend they were newcomers, to walk around and then to share what they saw. Their honest reflections were most helpful and became the basis for a project called Restoration 125, as part of our 125th anniversary. (I shared much of this story in my book *Come Let Us Build,* where I connect the story with Nehemiah.) The building restoration was done one job, one room, one floor at a time, from the exterior to the interior of the church sanctuary, followed by the lifting of the hall, and on to constructing a full basement and three-storey addition. Actually it was much more: it became a restoration of our heritage of service to the community. In this spirit we continued to expand, restore and build the Community Ministry Centre. There were moments of frustration, disappointment and bewilderment as the warning that these kinds of projects take twice the time and cost three times as much proved to be true. Such projects also bring out the best, the worst and the wackiest in people. However, the result was a very full, busy and beautiful facility.

The vision the Lord gave me was to reach out and serve the community from the streets to Parliament, from homes to businesses, and out to the nations, building the Kingdom of God.

One of the joys was the way God led me to partner with so many wonderful men and women in a wide variety of multi-layered ministries that flowed from our Community Centre. I don't take credit; they were the saints who made all this happen. Many ministries were launched, like a weekly lunch for seniors, a healing ministry, and a thrift store. In the end, our vision was fulfilled, many lives were touched, and the Kingdom was expanded.

God led us to the right people to see inter-church ministries established: Sanctuary Youth Centre was the vision of a former youth custody chaplain and began with the support of about nine local churches. Located in our basement, it provided a safe place for youth at risk to shower, have a hot meal, play pool, or just chat to one of the staff or many volunteers.

Leading Influence Ministries have office space in our Centre. Under the gifted leadership of the founding president, they provide chaplaincy service to our representatives at the Parliament Buildings down the road. He felt a call to this ministry and started showing up at Parliament, getting to know the staff and ministers alike. Soon he was well known so when the person meant to open one session in prayer didn't show up, he was invited to do so. Although no one has officially appointed him, he is effectively the chaplain to the members of Parliament. While he is developing such chaplaincies across the country, another pastor has now taken over this role in Victoria.

The Table, a congregation begun by two talented church planters, initially reached young adults. They now meet with all ages on Sunday afternoons, combining centralized worship services with neighbourhood groups, and have replanted another congregation on the Peninsula.

In 2012, COOL joined with another church that had lost its building. In the gym where they used to meet, a Sunday afternoon project providing a full meal for about one hundred fifty people called Living Edge was birthed. At the same time groceries are distributed from a downtown centre each week. This marketplace ministry has multiplied into nine distribution points strategically based around the city.

These are just a few of the local ministries. There were many more international missions, including exciting initiatives in Cuba and Malawi.

We did not escape scrapes along the way. One particularly difficult time involved an attempted coup. A small group decided they liked neither my leadership nor the direction we were going. They tried to take over leadership with the intention of getting rid of me. They seriously miscalculated, though, as the church rallied behind me. Dealing with such betrayal is incredibly hurtful, stressful and destructive. We have to learn to be gentle as doves but wise as serpents, to trust God not people. The Lord is our refuge, our present help in trouble. He is our rock, our shield, and our deliverer. He came through for me and the Church. I continue to look up and lift my hands in praise, for this is both our defensive and offensive strategy.

LOOK UP FOR OUR FUTURE

If we keep our eyes on God's eternal plan, His heavenly Kingdom, His heavenward direction, it completely changes the way we live on earth. By faith we are building God's Kingdom, which is not of this world, but has eternal significance. Hebrews 11 shows us that many heroes of the faith did not receive their promised reward in this life. God's purposes relate to His eternal Kingdom. Once we get this heavenly perspective, we'll be more effective in building an eternal legacy.

One of the characteristics of strong legacies in families is a sense of confidence which often grows from one generation to the next. This is good, but a different kind of confidence is needed in order to build a legacy for God's Kingdom. The Apostle Paul had all the usual confidence-builders like religious heritage, education, class, ethnicity and prestige, but he counted them as nothing in comparison to the one thing he valued more than anything, "...*the surpassing worth of knowing Christ Jesus my Lord*" (Philippians 3:8). This is where true confidence is found. As we get to know Him, we know more of ourselves, and have something to hand onto to others—a legacy.

God loves to take that which seems impossible and turn it around. If your family situation looks less than perfect, or even hopeless, don't despair. Keep praying and keep investing in their lives. Take hold of His covenant promises. Claim your family, your children, and your children's children for God's Kingdom. Let us pray those in our spiritual family would also continue that ripple effect and create waves.

We do this by sowing God's Word into their lives. God says,

> *Love the Lord Your God with all your heart and with all your soul and with all your strength. These commandments that I give you today are to be on your hearts. Impress them on your children. Talk about them when you sit at home and when you walk along the road, when you lie down and when you get up. Tie them as symbols on your hands and bind them on your foreheads. Write them on your doorframes of your houses and on your gates.* (Deuteronomy 6:5-9)

It is not easy to find ways to do this, not only because of busy schedules, but in the challenge of keeping the interest of children who have all kinds of distractions and excuses. Our family was no different and it meant adapting over the years. We tried to make devotion times enjoyable with stories and games, singing and dancing. We also insisted our children join us at church while they were at school. They knew that this was important to us and part of our daily and weekly activities. After that they could make their own choices and most went to other youth groups and churches at some point, but generally rejoined and supported us in our ministry.

We don't start out with an intention to build a legacy. This is a byproduct of other intentions, especially as we discover and follow God's purpose for our lives. Our service to God needs to be for its own sake and for His sake; the legacy will follow simply because He is good. Some of those who have a strong legacy in one area are equally deficient in other areas. The result is a disproportionate and imbalanced approach to life.

Questions

What makes some families strong in a certain field, leaving a legacy for generations? Are there any differences in leaving a legacy as a Christian?

Read Exodus 20:5, 6. Can we change the legacy of past generations by our own choices? Can we see the ripple effect of how we have or have not obeyed God's commands? How can we build a lasting legacy for our family and church?

Read Isaiah 51:1. Look back on your heritage, history, family, spiritual beginnings and how they have made you who you are today.

Read Isaiah 51:3. What are some examples of how God has turned our rubble and wasteland into a garden?

Read Isaiah 51:6. As you look up and forward, what do you see? What are your hopes for the future? What do you need to do today that will determine your legacy for tomorrow?

Pray for one another, for families and children, and for our spiritual families to continue to grow and leave a deposit for future generations.

CHAPTER 9
Balancing the Books

Accountants balance the books to ensure expenditures are accounted for and matched by income. Sometimes our life is out of balance, with too much expenditure of effort, resources and time without being replenished. God exhorts His people repeatedly that balance is essential to a life lived and finished well.

While many look for peace, harmony and balance in their lives, so often our primary preoccupation is simply to survive, seeking recreation in mostly hedonistic pleasures, and feeding our stomachs while our spirits starve. Most of us know we are too busy. Obesity has become a major concern in our Western culture, something that stems from a lack of balance in terms of physical activity and diet. Television has reduced us to spectators living vicariously through others' lives. The expectation of instant gratification often results in us being unable to cope with the stresses and strains of daily life, getting overhead in debt, and feeling dissatisfaction when reality bites.

I went to schools that sought to offer a balanced education. They succeeded in balancing the study program between the arts and sciences. We all had to do some form of creative arts, such as music or theatre. I peaked in Grade Five in my performance in *The Wizard of Oz*, in which I brilliantly played a tree. There was a spiritual component to my school. We had Assembly every morning with prayers and hymns. This was more of a formal duty than expressing a personal relationship with God, but still we were expected to go to church. We were meant to belong to a club of some kind. Of course, there was sport. You can tell how balanced was my approach: I played soccer followed by rugby, tennis, swimming, high board diving, cross-country and track. (My education was tilted more toward sport than anything else.) But as balanced an education as my school meant to provide, it fell short in overall life fulfillment.

True peace involves our whole being—body, soul, and spirit. *"May God himself, the God of peace, sanctify you through and through. May your whole spirit, soul, and body be kept blameless at the coming of the Lord"* (1 Thessalonians 5:23).

There will come a time of reckoning when we have to open our books and all our entries will be audited. This will be at the coming of the Lord. How will we be found? What does it mean and how does it work that our whole spirit, soul and body will be preserved blameless?

THE BODY

We cannot avoid the process of aging, which definitely includes a discouraging decline in our capacities and abilities. So much in today's culture is focused on physical beauty, looks, fashion, fitness, sex, gratification, diet, exercise and even extreme surgery like cosmetic surgery, all to make us look and feel good about ourselves. When we are young, we are probably more focused on the physical than anything else. As we get older these things should be less important, but in old age physical issues can take over in a different way. Now we complain about aches and pains, dental fixtures, long waits for new body parts and apparatus from knee and hip replacements to pacemakers and hearing aids.

Two New Testament Greek words clarify the relationship between the physical and spiritual: *soma* is the word used for our physical body, which is home to soul and spirit throughout our earthly lives. In this fallen existence, aging will eventually lead to physical death. *Sarx* refers to our fallen sinful nature with misdirected desires and lusts which lead to spiritual death. Paul cries, *"What a wretched man I am! Who will rescue me from this body that is subject to death?"* (Romans 7:24). Paul knows the solution as well, *"Thanks be to God, who delivers me through Jesus Christ our Lord"* (Romans 7:25).

Some significant events in the Christian calendar need to become our own personal experience of learning to live in our bodies.

On Good Friday we remember the death of Jesus, followed by Easter Sunday as we celebrate His resurrection. Part of our Christian experience is to be baptized into Jesus's death and resurrection (Romans 6:3,4). This frees us from sin so that when our earthly body *(soma)* dies, we can be resurrected into a new body for eternity. We also die to sin in our old fleshly nature *(sarx)* and are resurrected as new creatures while we continue our earthly journey. Our physical destiny is determined by being born again. Just as we are born physically, we have to be born spiritually. Jesus tells us, *"No one can see the kingdom of God unless they are born again"* (John 3:3). Thankfully, this new life is not dependent on us. It is a free gift of grace offered through God's covenant promise, fulfilled in Christ's finished work on the Cross. Because He has taken care of our sin, we can stand in His presence, justified—just as if we had not sinned. What follows is known as sanctification, the ongoing process of completion, perfection and preservation of our whole being.

Pentecost is when God manifested His presence by pouring out the Holy Spirit upon the early Church. We are baptized in the Holy Spirit in fulfillment of His promise, *"You will receive power when the Holy Spirit comes on you"* (Acts 1:8). This was my experience in Johannesburg. God the Holy Spirit enables and empowers us to make the right choices, helping us turn from sin to follow His way, and becoming equipped for ministry. Bishop Bill Burnett, a former Archbishop of Cape Town, had a great impact on my life. He was a regular churchman whose life was turned upside down by the Holy Spirit. One Sunday after lunch he was in his chapel in prayer when he heard the Lord telling him to give each part of his body over to Him. He offered his ears, eyes, and mouth, from the top of his head all the way down to his toes. He experienced an overwhelming outpouring of the Holy Spirit filling him to overflowing in the presence of the living Lord.

We are offered a similar opportunity during the Alpha course when Nicky Gumbel encourages us to offer every aspect of our life, including our bodies, gifts, time, ambitions, sexuality and finances to God during The Holy Spirit weekend. This weekend is pivotal, including as it does a transformative experience of complete surrender to the living God. We need not wait until we can participate in an Alpha course to do what God is always seeking from us, that we *"Offer your bodies as a living sacrifice, holy and pleasing to God—this is your true and proper worship"* (Romans 12:1).

THE SOUL

Psyche, meaning soul, is the root of the word psychology, which actually means study of the soul. Some confuse psychology with a secularized worldview. There is nothing wrong with psychology rooted in a Christian worldview and featuring a biblical theology. Some great psychologists like James Dobson and Larry Crabb are Christians. However, much of psychology is rooted in a secular humanistic worldview and ideology. Secular implies the denial of the transcendent and supernatural, accepting only that which can be verified by our senses. Humanism, the logical destination of secularism, is centred in humanity and sees human nature as basically good. Both these views deny the revelation of God about His perfect nature, and our imperfect sinful nature, as well as the reality of the eternal, not to mention His exclusive way to get there.

Jesus's death and resurrection is the only way our soul can be set free from sin to be resurrected into a new body, but also the only way we can truly live as fully human and godly beings. The Holy Spirit enables us to experience God's *shalom* in our mind, heart and will. It is part of the sanctification process where we need to "*Be transformed by the renewing of your minds. Then you will be able to test and approve what God's will is—His good, pleasing and perfect will*" (Romans 12:2). In other words, we can only exercise our free will in accordance with God's perfect will when our hearts and minds have been renewed by the Holy Spirit and have been brought into line with God's mind and heart. Being born again includes our soul.

The battleground for humanity begins when our hearts and minds are challenged by God's mind as expressed in His Word: "*Do not conform to the pattern of this world, but be transformed by the renewing of your mind*" (Romans 12:2).

The struggle with aging also begins in our minds, and for that as well, the solution begins in sharpening our minds. The phrase "Use it or lose it" applies very much to our brains. Whether through reading or writing, doing crossword puzzles or playing board games from Scrabble to chess, keeping the mind alert is as essential as keeping physically active. I prefer more physical activities than sitting at a table. One of the reasons I used to love squash so much was that while it was physically demanding, it also stretched me mentally. I constantly had to outthink and outsmart my opponent, which kept the old brain ticking. This is why regular participation in a sporting activity can increase our health in every way. Another activity I have grown to appreciate is dancing. Remembering the routines and sweating with the physical exertion, dancing is an excellent way of keeping young. It's important to find something that stretches us physically and mentally, and that we enjoy. Dutiful observance doesn't last as long as exuberant enthusiasm.

However, guarding and renewing our minds involves more than intellectual exercise.

There is a spiritual component to it.

THE SPIRIT

The spirit is the way we relate to the supernatural. As we are born again of the Spirit, we connect and commune with God, who is Spirit. *"God is spirit, and his worshippers must worship in the Spirit and in truth"* (John 4:24). But there are many gods and spirits with whom we can connect, and the Bible is full of references to them. We see people following different religions, often popularized by celebrities. The attraction they offer is a sense of spiritual fulfillment without the moral boundaries and expectations of a Father figure or the need for a Saviour. These are temporary illusions and don't lead to the true God or to His eternal destiny. In the Old Testament, God made it clear He expected absolute allegiance. *"I am the Lord your God... You shall have no other gods before me"* (Exodus 20:2,3). According to the New Covenant, there is only one path to get to God as offered by Jesus who says, *"I am the way and the truth and the life"* (John 14:6).

The Holy Spirit reassures us that we are God's children and heirs. We are provided with the resources to enjoy life in all its fullness and abundance, and to receive God's *shalom* in every part of our lives—spiritual, emotional, mental, social, relational, and economic. *"The Spirit himself testifies with our spirit that we are God's children"* (Romans 8:16). Jesus says, *"Peace I leave with you; my peace I give you"* (John 14:27). Peace is more than feeling; it is about being complete and whole. This is only possible in and through the Prince of Peace who breathes His Spirit into us. *"'Peace be with you! As the Father has sent me, I am sending you.' And with that He breathed on them and said, 'Receive the Holy Spirit'"* (John 20:21, 22).

When we are born again, God's Spirit infuses ours and we are connected for eternity. When we are baptized in the Spirit, we are immersed in that Spirit and are empowered for ministry. From this baptismal moment, God's commands are seen through different eyes. No longer are they inhibiting laws, but we recognize them as clear instructions from a caring Father for our well-being. Our God-given consciences are sharpened so that we know the difference between right and wrong as the Spirit writes these laws in our heart. They are not impossible demands but become part of our inner being, values and lifestyle. *"The Holy Spirit also testifies to us... 'This is the covenant I will make with them...' says the Lord. 'I will put my laws in their hearts, and I will write them on their minds'"* (Hebrews 10:16). We can see this in how our language can get cleaned up. As the Holy Spirit cleanses our heart and mind, we discover our vocabulary changes as well.

Like the human body, the Church is similarly made up as having a body and spirit. The organic relationship between us is referred to as the Body of Christ.

Each church has a distinctive spirit which should balance mind, emotion and will. Some churches will overemphasize one at the expense of the other. The spirit of the church needs to be infused with the Holy Spirit. The spirit can be damaged or enhanced by the history, experiences and theology in a church's life. As we gather corporately, united in one accord in worship, prayer, and fellowship, we open the door for God to breathe on us, filling us afresh in the Holy Spirit.

HOW DO WE RECEIVE THE HOLY SPIRIT?

Here are simple steps to prepare to receive the Holy Spirit.

1. Begin by breathing in and out.
2. The prime qualification for receiving the Holy Spirit is wanting Him. When we are so parched and thirsty to want Him more than anything else. "*Let anyone who is thirsty let him come to me and drink. Whoever believes in me...rivers of living water will flow from within them*" (John 7:37).
3. We can ask for Him. "*So I say to you: Ask and it will be given to you; seek and you will find; knock and the door will be opened to you...how much more will your Father in heaven give the Holy Spirit to those who ask Him*" (Luke 11:9, 13).
4. Repent as Jesus preached. Repentance means recognizing we are going in the wrong direction and need to turn away from all sin, and follow Jesus. This includes asking and receiving forgiveness for sins of our old nature, from greed to lust to anger to resentment to unforgiveness. Renounce any involvement with spiritual forces that are not the Holy Spirit, such as occult activities, astrology, clairvoyants, psychics, palm reading, playing with Ouija boards, etc.
5. Believe and Receive. In the 1970s, Colin Urquhart preached in our church in Cape Town, and described "coffee pot Christians" who come to receive from God but have the lid firmly in place. We have to take off the lid, open ourselves and receive. We thank God, believing we have received what we asked for, then acting by stepping out in faith and doing something. "*Therefore I tell you, whatever you ask for in prayer, believe that you have received it, and it will be yours*" (Mark 11:24).

Unless our spiritual needs are met by the God who is Spirit, we will never know true fulfillment and peace. However, as physical beings we live in a physical universe with physical needs. I now turn to what we usually mean by balancing the books: dealing with financial and economic issues. So much of our waking days are taken up with having a job, securing a roof over our heads, paying the rent or mortgage, putting food on the table, paying the bills, providing for our family, and meeting needs in our daily lives.

THE ECONOMY

One topic that takes up much of our working time and attention, adds to our stress, and causes endless conflict is finance. The economy is one of the most important areas of concern for society and governments at every level. Two opposing economic ideologies have been front and central around the world, capitalism and socialism. After a century of episodic failure, socialism is seeing a resurgence in the USA; it is an integral part of the 2020 election debate. So let's begin with this question: was Jesus a capitalist or socialist?

We are all aware that the world financial system has been through a huge meltdown in the last decade. Some blame capitalism, while others see socialism as a failed system. Most people are just wondering how they can survive. Which economic system is the most biblical? Jesus's feeding of the five thousand (John 6:1-15) reveals all. Here we see an familiar situation. Five thousand people are hungry. Jesus challenges the disciples to find a way to feed them. Andrew comes up with a young boy whose mom had packed him a brown bag lunch. How might a capitalist or socialist respond?

SOC THE SOCIALIST

Okay, we have five thousand mouths to feed, so let's take the fish and bread, and divide it up so each gets an equal share. As there isn't enough to go around, we then organize a picket outside the Roman Governor's office and demand a lunch program for educational and religious picnic events. They can tax somebody rich and set up a fish and sandwich supply store.

Like any ideology, there are pros and cons. The strength of socialism is the desire to share resources and to ensure the needy are taken care of. However, this should be something we do of our own volition, not by being compelled by a political system. More than that, socialism kills off the supply by giving it all away or cuts production taking so much by taxation. Socialism can lead to a poverty mentality in which poverty is seen to be a virtue, with the expectation that someone else will take responsibility for our provision. Among the many examples of countries going down this road, their economy dying, and people struggling to survive, are North Korea, Cuba, and Venezuela.

CAP THE CAPITALIST

Find out the little boy's name, then get Mom on the cell phone. Start baking bread. Organize Peter to get fishing. If you can do that net-on-the-other-side trick and fill it up, even better. Let's get busy. And I have a great idea for a side order—they're called fries.

Capitalism is all about supply and demand—the higher the demand, the higher the charge. *If it costs two denarii to cover the production cost of bread and fish, we need an eighty percent markup to clear a good profit. We have to pay the baker and the chef, marketing and advertising costs, transport and distribution, as well as build in profit for the entrepreneurial management. We'll sell each fish sandwich for ten denarii. Hey Jesus, do you want to be my partner? You draw the crowd, and I'll feed them. With that production thing you do, soon we can set up a franchise, the miracle fish shop. We can have one in Capernaum, another in Tiberius, still another in Beersheba, and maybe even Jerusalem.*

The strength of capitalism is that it employs people's skills to create wealth and provide for necessities. Its weakness is that it is open to abuse, exploitation and greed.

Greed mentality occurs when the focus is on more and more for me and mine, very often at the expense of someone else. This can be true of both socialism and capitalism because the root of the problem is more than any system. It is a condition of the heart called sin. Here are some of my greed grumbles.

PRIVATE SECTOR GREED

The 2008 collapse of the financial market, was caused in part by greed. From the misuse of corporate funds for exorbitant personal salaries and perks of many CEOs to the inflated and unrealistic expectations of both lenders and borrowers in the below-prime mortgage mess, greed played a major factor. Even before the collapse, financial institutions have long been rife with greed. Every quarter the banks post their billions of dollars in profits. When did we hear of them passing any break onto the consumer? Instead they increase their service and interest charges because their primary loyalty is to their shareholders. I may be a novice in economics, and I do believe in free enterprise, but there is something seriously wrong with such a system.

POLITICAL GREED

At federal and provincial levels of government, politicians ensure that they are well taken care of as they vote themselves generous salary increases with the rationale that this is the way to attract quality people to politics. The excessive salaries, perks and severance packages are examples of greed. We also see financial wrongdoing, gross mismanagement and waste.

PUBLIC SECTOR GREED

Many strikes by organized labour are a cause for concern. There are valid grievances, and collective bargaining is part of the process. But the greed factor is not far from the surface as the previously aggrieved become the aggressors.

CELEBRITY GREED

Thanks to television and movies, the entertainment industry can pay its stars obscene salaries beyond what most of us can imagine. Athletes, musicians, actors, and even some folk who seem to do nothing more than self-promotion are treated as celebrities. Tickets to games or concerts are raised beyond the ability of most ordinary workers. Scalpers escalate the gouging, buying up tickets with high tech robotic equipment to resell them at ever more exorbitant prices.

GAMBLING GREED

Gaming, as it is euphemistically called, is a social disease of epidemic proportions. The concept of wanting something for nothing ("Hey, you never know...") is a powerful attraction. Casinos continue to grow in popularity, along with social consequences such as addictions and crime. I know the rationale for lotteries is that they generate money for charity, but this is not a godly solution to financial needs. It is putting faith in chance. In fact I'll go so far as to say that it is a waste of money, even God's money.

Too many already hold the perception that the church only speaks about money, but how we deal with finance is one of the most important parts of discipleship. Money is a spiritual stronghold requiring spiritual eyes and resources to handle it.

ANOTHER WAY

Jesus operates on at least two levels when it comes to finances. He is the Lord to whom everything belongs; anything we have is by His grace. Also if we really believe He speaks to each of us, then He can be our financial manager or consultant.

When we invest money in the financial system, the obvious aim is to make more money. With the volatility in the markets and the uncertainty in the world today, it is a high-risk venture. It is prudent to be responsible in these matters and there are those more qualified than me to advise you. However, I can tell you one thing: there is another economy which is not subject to the vagaries of our fallen world, the economy of God's Kingdom.

I heard a story of a rich man who died soon after his servant. He was given a tour around heaven and was shown a mansion where his servant lived. He was greatly impressed as he thought, "Wow, if my servant lives in this mansion, mine must be incredible." When directed to his quarters, he was shocked to find he had been given a tiny little place the size of a closet. "There must be a mistake," he protested. He was told, "There's no mistake. This was all you sent up and so we didn't have much to work with." Like all illustrations this one has limitations. It merely illustrates a connection between what we offer while here, and what we are building for eternity. This illustration has lessons that apply to every area of our lives, including time and energy, possessions and money, family legacy, career and life. Whatever we offer to Him, He can use to build, create, grow, multiply.

We could call this way the Generous Giving Financial and Life Plan. Jesus said *"Do not store up for yourselves treasures on earth, where moths and vermin destroy, and where thieves break in and steal. But store up for yourselves treasures in heaven"* (Matthew 6:19-20). Jesus wants us to invest in God's Kingdom bank, but how do we do this?

God introduces this topic through the first fruits principle.

FIRST FRUITS

In the Old Covenant, many of God's promises to His people concern the Promised Land. He offers his children this land flowing with milk and honey for them to settle and enjoy. In return, he asks them: *"Bring the best of the firstfruits of your soil to the house of the Lord your God"* (Exodus 23:19). Again, God says, *"When you enter the land that I am going to give you and you reap its harvest, bring to the priest a sheaf of the first grain you harvest"* (Leviticus 23:10). In short, the best of the first fruit of our labour is offered to God in recognition that He is the provider, that He that has given all things to produce the harvest and to provide for the needs of His children.

In the New Covenant the only change is that God's offering is centred in the person of Jesus Christ: *"Christ, the firstfruits"* (1 Corinthians 15:23). In the gift of His One and only Son, God offers us His first and best. In return, He expects to be first in our lives as we offer our best to Him. This starts in our hearts. If God is first in my heart, if He is my first love, then everything else follows. This priority

impacts whatever we do, our time, energy and money. We offer the first fruit of the day in daily devotion, the first fruit of the week honouring the Sabbath in worship, and the first fruit of our labour in our financial offerings. When we follow God's direction to honour Him first, everything else falls into place; He is able to make the most of what we offer Him, with a good end result.

Giving the first fruit of our labour to God is a recognition that all we have is His, and that certainly includes money. The most common form of giving money is the tithe, which means giving God ten percent of our income off the top. In the Old Covenant, the tithe was usually divided into one third to the Levitical priesthood, one third to the temple, and one third to the poor. As a young Christian I was taught this principle and have put it into practice ever since. The New Covenant doesn't cancel the tithe. Rather the tithe provides a minimum guideline. We could give ten percent to our local church, and then offerings over and above that to missions. Or in line with the Old Covenant, we can tithe, giving two-thirds to our church and one third to mission and ministries. At COOL we gave ten percent to our denomination, which was our congregational church, and then another six percent to other missions.

When we don't tithe, we are actually robbing God. I didn't say that—God did:

> But you ask, 'How are we robbing you?' In tithes and offerings...Bring the whole tithe into the storehouse...Test me in this...and see if I will not throw open the floodgates of heaven and pour out so much blessing that there will not be room enough to store it. (Malachi 3:8-10)

As we give, everything falls into place. "*Whoever sows sparingly will also reap sparingly, and whoever sows generously will also reap generously...for God loves a cheerful giver*" (2 Corinthians 9:6, 7). We are called and are privileged to give generously, regularly and systematically. To summarize, God gave us His first and best, and considers us His first and best. He expects to be first and best in our lives and that we will offer our first and best to Him.

A prayer of David (2 Samuel 7:18-29) teaches us some helpful principles in this regard. David starts in humility: "*Who am I, Sovereign Lord, and what is my family, that you have brought me this far?*" (verse 18). He is grateful that God gives even more than he can imagine. David's next words—"*And as if this were not enough*" (verse 19)—show that he sees things in terms of God's purpose. He is overcome with praise, which is acknowledging God for who He is (verse 22). He

affirms his love for God's people and recognizes His redemptive purpose (verses 23-24). As in his encounter with Goliath, David's concern is for the honour of God's name (verse 26). He demonstrates a crucial principle by standing on God's revealed promises (verses 9-16) and praying them into reality. He asks with confidence, boldness and faith; his request is not based on his own selfish needs, but is for the blessing of the house, which is in line with God's promise. This is one of the primary keys to receiving answers to prayer. It is not a technique or formula but comes of a living relationship with a loving God, a working experience of His faithfulness to His Word.

Money is one of the big issues affecting our lives, rich and poor alike, and God is interested in how we treat it. In the next chapter we will apply the same principles to all kinds of health.

Questions

Describe areas of your life where there is balance and harmony, and areas where there is imbalance and disharmony.

How do we deal with the obsession with the physical in today's culture—from the beautiful houses to the beautiful people in magazines and television?

Read 1 Thessalonians 5:23. At the time of reckoning, the coming of the Lord, how will we be found? Look at John 3:3 and consider how being born again changes us in body, soul and spirit. How is this involved in our justification, our sanctification?

Read Romans 12:2. How can we align our hearts, minds and will with God's? Can we offer each part of our body and every aspect of our life specifically and intentionally to God?

Are we open to breathe and receive the Holy Spirit? Pray for one another to receive the Holy Spirit. Pray for your church to receive more of the Holy Spirit.

Do you have a stewardship/management plan? What is it? Which of these is closest to the way you live?

- We can go and find a corner to eat our fish and bread, maybe share it with our family, but the prime focus is on taking care of our own.
- We can be entrepreneurs and start a fish burger shop and make a lot of money.
- We can divide our fish and bread as far as it will go, but once it is finished, it's gone.
- We can offer all we have—our money and possessions, time and energy, talents and gifts, and invite Jesus to work miracles of reproduction growth.

How else can we balance our books?

CHAPTER 10

Taking Care of Our Health

While finances can concern us on regular basis, Canadians often place health care as their number one priority. We are blessed to have an excellent government-run health care system but at the same time there is a growing concern about unhealthy modern lifestyles. I believe we should all take responsibility for our own health to complement the medical system.

The apostle Paul describes us as temples of the Holy Spirit: "*Don't you know that you yourselves are God's temple and that God's spirit dwells in your midst? If anyone destroys God's temple, God will destroy that person; for God's temple is sacred, and you together are that temple*" (1 Corinthians 3:16, 17). This description of us as God's temple includes the corporate body of the Church, and our individual bodies, souls and spirits in which God has chosen to dwell by His Spirit. While this primarily means we should live godly lives, I want to broaden the application to include taking care of ourselves physically.

All of us have been given our bodies as a gift, with different genetic makeup, skills and abilities, shapes and sizes. I return to a psalm we have looked at before because it speaks to our physical bodies, Psalm 139. God has taken great trouble to create each of us individually and uniquely as we are. Who are we to complain?

God's part and gift to us is the making of our bodies. Our responsibility is to be good managers and to make the most of what we have been given. I see three different perspectives addressing that responsibility. First, prevention is better than cure, and keeping in shape is a good prescription for generally healthy living. Second, we live in a fallen world where illness is a reality; there are those who live with debilitating disability and disease. Last but not least, we worship the God who heals.

PREVENTION IS BETTER THAN CURE

As we approach middle age, most of us delay facing our diminishing physical abilities and expanding waistlines.

I have always loved sports and played regularly but I also had a sweet tooth with a penchant for ensuring that everything on the table received equal attention. Junk food was a treat and meals were not complete without dessert. As I entered middle age, though, I began to spread in those areas that many middle-aged men spread. On the other hand, Lynne is not naturally sporty but she loves all the right foods with lots of green vegetables and salads. We know that in order to keep healthy, three elements are required: good diet, regular exercise, and a good night's sleep. Parents teach children to brush their teeth, comb their hair, wash, and other such basic physical requirements. Although most adults have the hang of these actions, we need to add some physical behaviours to our daily routine and lifestyle, particularly exercise and healthy eating habits.

New Year's resolutions often reflect the importance of health. I recorded my own specific goals regarding my weight over time. In 1985, I weighed 184 pounds and wanted to get to 180; in 1990, I weighed 190 and wanted to get to 185; in 1995, I weighed 195 pounds and wanted to get to 190; in 2002, I weighed 199 pounds and set a goal of 195 pounds. Many people will identify with this puzzling phenomenon of weight going in the wrong direction. On the one hand, we can rationalize that this is just inescapable middle-aged spread. On the other hand, why should we accept it?

In 2004, something changed for me. While I have always enjoyed sport and exercise, my eating habits did not get the same attention. I got serious about making some changes. I learned that carbohydrates and sugars turn to fat and clog the arteries. I made an intentional choice to cut these down in my diet and to eat more healthy meals. This meant salads instead of fries, water instead of pop, vegetables instead of bread, and drastic reduction of desserts, cake and ice cream. I lost fifteen pounds in about two months, eventually losing another five before settling into my ideal weight of 180 pounds. I had turned the clock back nearly three decades. Over the years I have had some slip-ups and have put on an extra pound or two, but I am pleased to say that at seventy years old, my weight is still 180 pounds.

At the same time, I incorporated a disciplined routine of daily exercise rather than sporadic attempts. Each of us needs to find something we enjoy doing and build it into our daily routine. Walk, hit a ball, do some simple exercises, or find a sport. I used to play an hour's hard squash twice a week and swim one hundred lengths of a twenty-five metre pool twice a week. As my joints started to object, I reluctantly hung up my squash racquet after forty years. As a replacement, I discovered the sport of pickleball, a sort of old timer's tennis, strangely named after the founder's dog. With its own peculiar terminology and special rules, pickleball has developed a huge following, especially among seniors. It is great fun and good exercise.

I continue swimming lengths and doing a weekly "mini-triathlon" training routine which included the bike and treadmill in the gym and lengths in the pool. Eventually I may not be able to keep up with this regimen and I'll need to make more adjustments. A shoulder injury has resulted in me doing more breast stroke and less free or fly (over-arm) strokes in the pool. The important thing is to keep active as best we can. I watch people in their nineties still shuffling up to the pool edge and continuing to swim. They may not be as fast or do as much as they once did, but they keep going.

Men are notorious for avoiding doctors, yet physicians are essential partners in our heath care. My annual physical gives me the information I need to take charge of my health, such as my best body mass index, blood pressure, and cholesterol. The latter was too high and needed concentrated attention; changing more of my favourite foods became necessary for good health. I also reluctantly accepted my doctor's advice to start taking a small amount of medication to help. I am now in as good a shape as ever and can out-run, out-swim, out-play, out-think, out-smart and out-last many men half my age. (Of course I say that with the utmost humility, perhaps some denial, and with less confidence each year.)

I am fully aware that we can take nothing for granted, and that every breath and every second is a gift from God which can be taken away without notice. But my responsibility is to play my part in keeping myself in the best physical shape possible. I need to take personal responsibility for my own health care system and be a good steward of God's gift of life to me. I want to encourage you to do the same and take pro-active preventative measures to keep healthy.

LIVING WITH DISABILITY

We are also part of a fallen universe where disease and aging are part of the process. Lynne's experience is very different from mine, but one with which many will identify. With severe health challenges over the years, she has experienced miraculous healing on the one hand, but has also had to learn to live with disability and limited physical capabilities.

Lynne has not been active in sports but is slim and looks younger than her age. She did engage in aerobic exercise and occasionally swam with me but a disabling neurological problem put an end to all that. In high school, Lynne suffered from the eating disorder anorexia, perhaps as a way of dealing with stresses in her life. We are not sure whether this was the cause but health challenges have followed her throughout her adult life.

I have shared the challenges we had falling pregnant, but one of her most severe health problems occurred during her pregnancy with our youngest daughter in 1986. In the latter stages of pregnancy, she fell and injured her pelvis. It was then discovered she had severe osteoporosis. After our daughter's birth, Lynne's condition deteriorated and she shuffled around like an old woman. We had many people praying for her, but one night I dragged her to a healing service with Benny Hinn. The service went on and on. I questioned much of his theology, and both of us were ready to give up and go home. Just then he began to pray for the sick with words of knowledge. He pointed directly at Lynne and said there was a woman suffering in a lot of pain from a serious bone condition, but that the Lord was healing her. At that moment the anointing of the Holy Spirit came upon Lynne. Over the next few months she made a choice not to be sick and to get active. She began to teach drama at a school, her strength slowly came back and her bones showed a marked improvement

John Wimber and a Vineyard team came to Cape Town. During a prayer time, one of the Vineyard pastors spoke a word about Lynne having scoliosis. As we prayed, her back straightened up and she was healed. For many years she was much better.

Soon after beginning our ministry at Church of Our Lord, Lynne became the British Columbia Director of Scripture Union. In spite of having a terrible cold and flu which developed into pneumonia and encephalitis, she insisted on going to Missionfest in Vancouver. Upon her return, her health deteriorated so severely that she couldn't walk for about seven months. Attempts to diagnose the problem evaded the doctors until one South African doctor suggested she might have a condition called antiocardolipin antiphospholipid syndrome, defined by the presence of abnormal antibodies. Once again, a combination of prayer, Lynne's determination, and the Lord's healing resulted in her slow improvement.

Lynne's most recent serious illness occurred at the beginning of 2018 when she contracted shingles. At first, this did not seem to be a serious bout as she only had a small rash which did not last long. We went away on vacation, but in the last week she suddenly began to experience excruciating pain in her hips. Once again it seemed the medical system had difficulty making a diagnosis, but doctors eventually concluded this was post-herpetic neuralgia with bursitis. More than a year later, she was slightly improved but still had major mobility issues when she fell, tearing ligaments and muscles in her hip.

The restriction on her activities is extremely frustrating and difficult but I want to share with you that Lynne has not let any of these struggles get in the way of fulfilling her call as a Bible teacher, pastor and involved grandmother. No matter how poorly she has slept, how much pain she feels, or how difficult things may be, she will get up and go to honour her commitments.

Two well-known Christians have incredible testimonies of not allowing the cards they have been dealt rob them of making the most of their lives. Joni Erikson Tada has lived as a quadriplegic since a diving accident as a young woman put her in a wheelchair. She went through all the emotions of grief, anger, confusions and doubt, sought healing that never came, but in the end came to a place of acceptance of who she is in Christ. She was able to testify of His sovereignty and Lordship in her condition and has become an inspiration for multitudes through her writing about her life.

The other is a man born with tetra-amelia syndrome, a rare disorder characterized by the absence of arms and legs. This is not exactly the start in life most us would wish for, yet Nick Vujicic did not let life without limbs become a stumbling block. Nick has shown his adventurous spirit by engaging in many activities some of us with all our limbs would never try. Nick is married with four children and has become a sought-after speaker whose message inspires millions. Instead of feeling sorry for himself or seeing himself as a victim, Nick gives a powerful testimony of his belief in Jesus Christ and God's purpose for his life.

Both Joni and Nick are living examples of this much-quoted verse, "*And we know that in all things God works for the good of those who love Him, who have been called according to His purpose*" (Romans 8:28). God is in the redemption business working out His purpose.

When we hear of people who say they can't attend church or house group because of the weather, fatigue, or some other weak excuse, it is nothing compared to the effort folk like Joni and Nick have to go through to get out the door. We had some folk at COOL who were an example to everyone. A ninety-plus lady used to walk six blocks to church come rain, snow or whatever. Another tough lady in a wheelchair maneuvered herself with great difficulty but was also one of our most committed disciples. What made the difference? They had desire, devotion, commitment and endurance because Jesus was truly Lord of their lives.

When we are feeling sorry for ourselves that our age is catching up with us, what can we do? The best antidote to our sedentary aging process is to get active. Here are some simple yet often doable steps:

Ask: Knock, ask, and seek the Lord with all our heart, mind, will and strength. Come and bring all our health needs to the Lord who heals.

Trust: Trust in the Lord who answers our prayers. *"And my God will meet all your needs according to the riches of His glory in Christ Jesus"* (Philippians 4:19). And remember, *"I can do all this through him who gives me strength"* (Philippians 4:13).

Get Physical: We can make the most of whatever our condition, be it good health or poor health. We can ensure that we are eating healthy foods by re-training our taste buds, and finding methods exercise we enjoy. Walking is one of the most inexpensive, enjoyable and healthy exercises nearly everyone can do.

Rejoice: *"Rejoice in the Lord always. I will say it again: Rejoice"* (Philippians 4:4).

THE LORD WHO HEALS

I am a little hesitant to mention healing. I have been put off by the sensationalist approach, the "Come and get your miracle today!" approach, and I hate seeing people disappointed if they are not healed. On the other hand, I have always believed in healing and in praying for my own family I have seen God's healing power at work.

When one of our daughters was playing in her mother's high heel shoes, she tripped down the stairs. Her ankle swelled up as she cried in pain. Lynne and I immediately prayed over her in the spirit. Within a few minutes the swelling disappeared and she was back to playing. On another occasion, my father was in hospital after a coronary, looking like he was dying. I had a sense this was not his time to die and prayed for the Lord to heal him. The next day he was completely restored and went on to live a good many years before he was called home. My mother was in bad shape in hospital with pneumonia when my sister and I prayed over her one evening; by the next day the difference was remarkable.

Over the years we have seen many wonderful healings beyond our family. I remember being called to the hospital late one night to pray for one of our dear church members who suffered from obstructive pulmonary disease. Her main symptom was difficulty in breathing. A fellow church leader and I anointed her with oil and prayed over her for about an hour; we prayed her back from the grave to life. Later she jokingly chastised me for not letting her go to be with the Lord. A year later she had another attack and this time I did pray for her to be relieved from this suffering and she took her last breath before passing to heaven where she was free from her suffering body. I long to see people freed from the physical, emotional, relational, spiritual burdens that just drain vitality and productivity. I am happy to let God decide how He will achieve their freedom.

I frequently return to this central verse: *"For God so loved the world that He gave His one and only Son, that whoever believes in Him shall not perish but have eternal life"* (John 3:16). Perish is an interesting word that means rot and decay, die and destroy. It includes our physical and spiritual condition, as well as our eternal situation. God has an interest in both. Jesus came to save the world from sin that prevents us from having a personal relationship with a holy and loving God. He also healed people from diseases, which are simply consequences of living in a sinful world.

Healing is part of the very nature of God Himself, as we read in Exodus, *"For I am the Lord, who heals you"* (Exodus 15:26). On the Cross, the finished work of Jesus includes our salvation and our healing. Matthew quotes Isaiah 53:4, *"He took up our infirmities and bore our diseases"* (Matthew 8:17), while Peter writes, *"...by his wounds you have been healed"* (1 Peter 2:24). This means that the basis for healing is established by Jesus's work on the Cross.

This world is occupied by a usurping power, Satan, otherwise known as *"the god of this age"* (2 Corinthians 4:4). Jesus came to take on the powers of this world to inaugurate the Kingdom and rule of God, *"Now is the time for judgment on this world; now the prince of this world will be driven out"* (John 12:31). At salvation, we are transferred from the one kingdom to the other. Jesus challenges all hearers: "Repent for the kingdom of heaven has come near" (Matthew 3:2). The author of Colossians describes it like this: *"For he has rescued us from the dominion of darkness and brought us into the kingdom of the Son he loves"* (Colossians 1:13).

Jesus is the Lord of all creation who has demonstrated His power over nature, disease and even death. He shows both His ability and His willingness to heal the sick. He responds to the leper's request, *"Lord, if you are willing, you can make me clean*" (Luke 5:12) by reaching out His hand, touching the man, and saying, "*I am willing...be clean!*" (Luke 5:13)

At the same time, we know that not all are healed. Honestly, I don't know all the reasons why. I do know that we live in a fallen universe which falls short of God's perfect standards and intentions. The reality is that our bodies are decaying, aging and dying. There is a whole industry to delay the inevitable, from diets and exercise to cosmetic surgery. As I mentioned, it is important to have our own plan for keeping healthy but disease may hasten the inevitable and likewise impede our best efforts. God sometimes intervenes and delays the process.

How does this intervention happen? For one thing, our bodies have natural healing components built in to their systems. For example, when we cut ourselves, if we clean the wound, along with natural components in the body, our body will recover. In the same way medicine works together with the body to heal. Prayer sometimes works in the same way, in partnership with our bodies, and with God Himself, as Creator, Saviour and Rescuer. God also works miracles in ways that cannot be explained in terms of partnership with our limited capacities. The bottom line is that with God it really is all good.

God's overall purpose and priority is for all of us to spend eternity with Him. Dealing with the sin that prevents life is His main concern. The Gospel is His solution and salvation plan. But it also includes us having abundant life here and now.

As disciples we are also called to follow Him and do what He did—pray for the sick. Let's look at three principles for praying for the sick.

COME

"*There some people brought to him a man who was deaf and could hardly talk, and they begged Jesus to place his hand on him*" (Mark 7:32). This scene shows us one principle: a person comes to Jesus or someone comes to Jesus on their behalf. They ask Him to heal the person. We can see this in other biblical examples, such as the men who brought their paralyzed friend on a stretcher, climbed onto the roof, dug a hole and let him down (Luke 5:17-26). There was the Syrophoenician woman who fell at Jesus feet and begged Him to deliver her daughter (Matthew 15:21-28). Others include Jairus who pleaded on behalf of his dying daughter, the Jewish elders who came on behalf of a Roman centurion asking for his servant's healing, and the blind beggar who cried out, "*Son of David, have mercy on me*" (Mark 10:48).

In a story, Jesus commended a person who showed persistence in knocking on his neighbour's door until midnight to get some bread for his children. *"Ask and it will be given to you; seek and you will find; knock and the door will be opened to you"* (Matthew 7:7). We come, we bring, we ask!

TOUCH

"Jesus put His finger into the man's ears. Then he spit and touched the man's tongue" (Mark 7:33). He did the same with a blind man. This may seem strange and unhygienic to us, yet it is in this dramatic act of touch that Jesus's power heals. The woman who reached out to touch Jesus's robe created the same release of power (Luke 8:43-48). Touch is sacramental in this way, an outward sign of an inward reality or grace, a visible demonstration of a healing act. It is the same as laying on hands or anointing with oil. James instructs us:

> *Is anyone among you sick? Let them call the elders of the church to pray over them and anoint them with oil in the name of the Lord. And the prayer offered in faith will make the sick person well; the Lord will raise them up.* (James 5:14, 15)

These outward signs don't heal in themselves, but they are the catalyst for God's power to connect with our faith in order to release His healing power. Holy Communion is another sacramental occasion when we receive God's power to meet our needs, especially healing. Once again, we are called to come to Him.

Just as our hands give, protect, work, create, cover, bless and heal, the Lord's hand is upon us; we need only reach out and take it. *"The Lord's right hand is lifted high; the Lord's right hand has done mighty things!"* (Psalm 118:16). It is just as important that we are willing to reach out to touch someone in His Name.

SPEAK

The spoken word releases the power of God's creative Word, *"My word...will not return to me empty, but will accomplish what I desire and achieve the purpose for which I sent it"* (Isaiah 55:11). In healing the deaf man, *"He looked up to heaven, and with a deep sigh said to him 'Ephphatha!' (which means, 'Be opened!')"* (Mark 7:34).

Words have the power to destroy or create and, when infused with the Holy Spirit, the power to heal. Jesus says to the paralytic whose sins He forgave to get up and go home. (Mark 2:11). He says to Jairus's daughter, *"Little girl, I say*

CHAPTER 11

Developing Our EQ

We've covered finance, health, so now how about we take a look at our emotions? Emotions are something men tend to avoid even more than they do the doctor. One thing we notice in both society and the Church is the absence of skills for dealing with relationships, pressure, conflicts and challenges in a mature way. At the roots of the problem are family and social structures that have lost their foundation and direction. In the delusion of freedom, children are growing up without understanding the security of boundaries or the benefits of self-discipline and delayed gratification. Wanting it all now is the cry of the day. The result is immature self-centredness.

People seem increasingly unable to be mature and confident managers of their own lives, let alone to develop healthy relationships with a spouse, parent, sibling, friends and neighbours, employees or employers. Increasingly we see dysfunctional people and families, which in turn leads to a dysfunctional society. God is passionately interested in our psyche or soul, and our relationships, both functional and dysfunctional. We often need a good chat with both our soul, and God, as exemplified in the Psalms. "*Why, my soul, are you downcast? Why so disturbed within me? Put your hope in God, for I will yet praise Him, my Savior and my God*" (Psalm 42:5).

WHAT IS EQ?

Our emotional quotient or EQ is as important as our Intelligence Quotient or IQ. The term EQ was popularized by Daniel Goleman in 1995, and has been described as an ability, capacity or skill to perceive, assess and manage the emotions of oneself, others and social groups.

Four characteristics of the EQ are: self-awareness—knowing and recognizing our feelings; self-management—handling feelings and reacting appropriately; social awareness—recognizing and responding to feelings in others; and, social management—handling interpersonal relationships.

God's salvation includes spiritual regeneration of our body, soul and spirit. When we focus only on one of these, it leads to an imbalance. All around us we can see the results of carnal bondage due to this imbalance. Some are so soul-driven that their faith is over- intellectualized, emotional, or will-powered. Others fall to a form of spiritual elitism where everything is spiritualized while their personal lives are a disaster. All of us need to come under the regenerative, balancing power of the Holy Spirit.

When the EQ is under-developed, soul life seems to stall without developing to maturity. We may have difficulty in sustaining long term relationships, stumbling from one broken relationship to another, taking offense at the slightest issue. Others manipulate, control and bully to get their own way. Still others can't cope with boundaries or self-control, looking for love in all the wrong places. We can see some of these characteristics in car drivers: the person who shows no awareness or consideration for other drivers will probably relate in the same way in other situations. We have all come across people who are so focused on their own agenda that they have no awareness of anyone else's feelings. Sadly, this sometimes applies to Christians.

In the last chapter we examined getting in shape physically. Now we are looking at growing and maturing our souls and our hearts.

Lent is a seasonal reminder that overcoming temptation is a prerequisite to growth in maturity. Just as Jesus was led into the desert, at some point in our own spiritual journey most of us will be led into the wilderness for testing as part of our growth. Sport can teach us similar principles. Learning how to win and lose with grace and endurance, overcoming conditions and emotions, relating to teammates and opponents, having the right winning attitude, and so on.

Lynne and I enjoy watching reality TV shows such as the *Amazing Race* and *Survivor* not only to see the beautiful travel locations, but also because we are fascinated by the complex dynamics of human relationships. We see sinful nature at its worst as people connive, manipulate and deceive to get ahead. Sadly this whole scenario has certain similarities with life in general, and even the ministry.

In more forty years of ministry and involvement with at least two major building projects, I saw the best, the worst and the wackiest in people. The way people, including Christians, react to challenges, difficulties and problems is incredibly illuminating. I have observed and been on the receiving end of a wide range of human behaviour. These kinds of interactions are helpful to our learning curve, but the best teacher is the Word of God which is "*alive and active. Sharper than any double-edged sword, it penetrates even to dividing soul and spirit...it judges the thoughts and attitudes of the heart*" (Hebrews 4:12).

GROWING IN MATURITY

Developing our EQ is closely related to growing in maturity. Ephesians 4 presents us with a number of personal awareness and management principles that help us grow in this area.

BE HUMBLE (EPHESIANS 4:2)

The starting point is recognition that we are not the centre of the universe. When we know Jesus, He becomes the centre. Humility begins by submission to Him, and then that flows into submission to one another. It means submitting my desires and putting someone else first. It does not mean a false humility in which we think we have nothing to offer. In fact, true humility comes from having a confidence and assurance about who we are in Christ and being able to give without expecting anything in return.

"BE STEADFAST"

Long-suffering means being able to suffer and overcome over the long haul. When a number of followers quit, Jesus asked his disciples whether they would also give up. They answered, "*To whom shall we go? You have the words of eternal life*" (John 6:68) Where we start is important, but where we finish is even more so. Completing our mission with reliability, working through issues, seeing problems as opportunities, overcoming challenges and holding fast are all important personal management requirements.

A person for whom I once had respect deserted his post over a doctrinal issue. He had every right to stand for his beliefs but instead of sitting down and working out the best response for all concerned, he cut and ran. Whatever the right and wrong of the principles in question, this way of dealing with a disagreement causes much damage. If, after working through the issues together, there is a recognition of no agreement and that the best solution is to part ways, then hopefully it can be done with mutual agreement and blessing. This is a better way.

"STAND FIRM"

Closely related to steadfastness is the ability to stand firm, offering stability and security in all circumstances. The only way to do this is to have our feet firmly planted on the Rock, in God's Word. Then we won't be tossed to and fro by the latest fad, doctrine or anything else that comes to knock us off our feet. We need to know the Word, know God the Father, Son, and Holy Spirit, know the tactics of the enemy, know ourselves and our strengths and weaknesses, and even know the fickleness of human nature. The good news is these are all available in the pages of the Bible. Jesus overcame temptation in the wilderness by quoting Scripture, not in a pat way, but by knowing the power of God's words which reflected His mind, will and desires. Let our yes be yes and our no be no. Show integrity by being decisive, resisting evil and overcoming temptation.

"SPEAK THE TRUTH IN LOVE" (EPHESIANS 4:15)

As we hear the truth, we need to take responsibility for our own decisions rather than blaming others or getting sucked into a victim mentality. Walking the road to maturity means making the most of circumstances, being thankful for what we have and not complaining about what we don't have.

As we experience the *shalom* peace of God, resting in His perfect will, seeking the Lord with all our heart and becoming more aware of God in all His fullness, we will grow in self-awareness, maturity and responsibility. When we start our children or a new employee on a path, we slowly increase their responsibilities as they develop their ability to cope. God does the same with us.

INTERPERSONAL/SOCIAL AWARENESS AND MANAGEMENT

The term "one another" comes up in the Bible over and over again. God views how we treat one another as a priority. Four of the Ten Commandments are about our relationship with God; six are about our relationships with one another.

"BEAR WITH ONE ANOTHER...IN LOVE" (EPHESIANS 4:2)

This involves putting into practice all of the above with one another, whether it is our children going through their difficult phases, parents as they age, fellow members in the church, or anyone who gives us a hard time. It is the practical outworking of being patient, steadfast and long-suffering, and one of the many dynamics of love. Our responsibility is to help build up rather than tear down. Many emotional and relational problems stem from not bearing with one another in love. We hold onto grievances, resentments, anger, guilt, grief and other legitimate emotions, but without bringing them to God for resolution.

SERVE ONE ANOTHER (EPHESIANS 4:12)

Ministry means service. In any relationship, we are called to serve one another's needs. This is one of the signs of true maturity, when we start to take our eyes off ourselves and look to the interests of others. We don't need to wait for them to ask. We seek to be sensitive to their needs and serve them. We are to be faithful in the small things, serving one person at a time. A good learning place is in prayer meetings and Bible studies. There we can learn to listen to what is being said, be sensitive to others, not overpower anyone else, and live in harmony together.

"SPEAKING THE TRUTH IN LOVE" (EPHESIANS 4:15)

We all need to learn this principle of speaking the truth in love. Some people are very direct, but lack love. Others are very loving but find it hard to be firm.

I have found helpful the PAC model for transactions and communication. P stands for Parent, A for Adult, and C for Child. When we operate from a child-parent dynamic, we play victim and manipulation games. Parent-child is about control and bullying. We need to learn to interact with one another adult to adult. This means being firm, direct, and honest, telling it like it is with no nonsense on the one hand, and being sensitive, gracious and graceful on the other.

Are we naturally willing to receive correction and admonishment in a loving environment? Sadly, some take offense and become defensive, while many take the line of least resistance by immediately cutting off relationship.

GROWING IN EQ MATURITY

If we want to grow up in maturity, developing our emotional quotient, we need to grow in two ways:

GROW INTO THE HEAD (EPHESIANS 4:15)

If Jesus is the head of the body of Christ, then He is the one who gives thought, clear direction, commanding the movement of all the limbs in the body. Without

Him, we can do nothing. As we remain or abide in Him, His life-giving Spirit flows in and through us, and we are renewed in our way of thinking so we can have the very mind of Christ.

The head and body are inextricably attached. A body cannot live if it is decapitated, although spiritually speaking, many try to live as though they can. Some claim to believe in Jesus but will have nothing to do with His Body, the Church. But if we truly grow up into the Head and into maturity, we need to recognize that we are part of His Body.

GROW TOGETHER IN THE BODY (EPHESIANS 4:16)

God's plan is that through relationship with one another, through the exercising of gifts so that we can be properly equipped, and through growing together in organic unity, together we will grow up in maturity. This is not going to happen in the isolated world of me and mine. As challenging, offensive and annoying as people can be, we need one another. No pain, no gain. Are we up for God to help us grow together as the Body of Christ?

The older we get the more set in our ways we become. Our souls and our hearts can become hardened by the wear and tear of disappointments and dissatisfactions. A good chat with our soul is an important reality check. But without the intimate involvement of a transcendent yet involved and loving God, it will be a self-serving exercise. The wisdom of our heavenly Father, the saving grace of our Lord Jesus Christ, and the softening touch of the Holy Spirit will enable our soul to mature so that we can grow sweeter and more gracious instead of more sour and bitter.

Part of growth in emotional maturity involves recognizing that there has to be change, and that change starts with ourselves.

Questions

Read Psalm 42:5. Have you ever had a chat with your soul? What would you say?

What would you like to say to "God your Rock" about your soul condition?

Can you remember the description of emotional quotient?

How can we become more aware of self and others? Read Hebrews 4:12. What does dividing the soul from the spirit mean? How are our skills in managing ourselves and others?

Read 1 Corinthians 3:1-3. How can we protect ourselves from slipping into the Corinthian church's immaturity?

Read Ephesians 4:13. How can we *become mature, attaining to the whole measure of the fullness of Christ?"*

Where do we need to grow in integrity so our yes can be yes and our no be no? (Matthew 5:37)

The tragic lives and deaths of celebrities attract our interest and concern. How could an underdeveloped emotional quotient be the cause of their problems? If you are in a group, discuss.

CHAPTER 12

Changing Our Patterns

There is a saying, attributed to Henry Ford, "If you always do what you've always done, you'll always get what you've always got." It is also said, "You can't teach an old dog new tricks." Are we aging older dogs destined to be stuck in our ways? If we are to mature and grow, it involves change as surely as new wine requires new wineskins.

Change is at the heart of being alive, but more importantly, of being a follower of the living God. There are many incredible stories of changed lives in the Bible, none more dramatic than that of a con man named Jacob.

FROM CON MAN TO OVERCOMER

How does a cunning con man and conniving trickster get to be God's chosen agent? How does a momma's boy get to be the father of God's people? How does a soup swindler get to be a wrestling champion? How does Jacob, the deceiver, become Israel, the one who has struggled with God and overcome?

I sometimes wonder what was God thinking with Jacob. What does this story say about God, about what pleases Him? Jacob was a rather unsavoury character, and yet he is a textbook example of how God in His grace can choose the most unlikely material and mould us into something great for His purpose.

Jacob illustrates God's care, forgiveness, and transformation working overtime. His track record in Genesis reads like a rollercoaster. Jacob is at the bottom as he tricks Esau (Genesis 25) and deceives his father (Genesis 27). He rides to the top with his vision at Bethel (Genesis 28), hits the bottom again in his squabbles with Laban (Genesis 29) and the jealousy between his wives (Genesis 30), and goes up again in his wrestling encounter at Peniel (Genesis 32) and reconciliation with Esau (Genesis 33). I invite you to read all the chapters to get the whole story.

In Hebrew custom, the firstborn son would receive a double portion of the inheritance. Jacob and Esau were direct heirs of their grandfather Abraham's covenant promises, and it was Esau's responsibility as the eldest to ensure they continued. Esau was the outdoorsy type, hunting, fishing and shooting. He was a man's man, his father's favourite. Jacob was the quiet, indoor, nerdy type who stayed at home and was his mother's favourite. So in the case of birthrights and blessings, how did Jacob end up with both, and Esau with nothing?

Esau gives us an example of the gimme generation, although such people have been around since the Garden of Eden. "*Quick, let me have some of that red stew! I am famished*" (Genesis 25:30). He says. He demands immediate gratification and puts his own immediate physical needs above his long term spiritual responsibilities. Esau despised his birthright, showing complete disregard for God's priorities, while Jacob was the opposite, holding the birthright and blessing in such high esteem that he was willing to do anything to get them. "*First sell me your birthright*" (Genesis 25:31), Jacob demands. He goes on to impersonate his brother and lies through his teeth to their aging and essentially blind father, telling him he is Esau (Genesis 27:19). God seems to overlook his dubious methods in favour of the intentions of his heart. Jacob's mother, Rebekah, was the driving force behind the deception, but Jacob showed the determination to ask and fight to receive. "*Please sit up and eat some of my game, so that you may give me your blessing*" (Genesis 27:19).

What does this tell us about God? For openers, His choices and His ways are different from ours. Where we look at the outward appearance and the obvious, God sees the heart. In fact, God even goes so far as to say, "*Jacob I loved, but Esau I hated*" (Romans 9:13). In Hebrew idiom, this is more of an expression of preference than what we mean as hate, but why? We know that Esau made two major mistakes:

• He assumed his privilege as the elder brother. Israel often fell into the same trap of claiming entitlement to God's covenant blessing while neglecting the responsibility that went with it.

- He also showed no acknowledgment of his sin. He was remorseful for what he had lost and wanted to take out his anger on his brother, rather than repenting to make things right with God. There were long-lasting consequences to this anger. Esau's descendants, the Edomites, were in constant conflict with Israel and on the receiving end of God's judgment.

Playing the blame game is the root of many social problems and even movements today. Instead of taking responsibility, with its potential to actually make a difference, we blame others from government, to society, and from history to family, expecting someone else to fix our problems. One dimension of growing into maturity is focusing on other's needs before our own, serving rather than expecting to be served. The starting place is worshiping God.

A New Testament story about a shrewd manager (Luke 16) seems rather strange yet has a similar message to that of Jacob's story:

Whoever can be trusted with very little can also be trusted with much, and whoever is dishonest with very little will also be dishonest with much. So if you have not been trustworthy in handling worldly wealth, who will trust you with true riches? And if you have not been trustworthy with someone else's property, who will give you property of your own? (Luke 16:10-12)

Jesus uses this story as an example of fitness for spiritual blessings. If we cannot manage what we have been given in the physical realm, we can hardly expect God entrust to us with His heavenly spiritual gifts and power.

Jacob's methods can certainly be questioned, but it was his desire, intent and commitment that God honoured. Esau wanted personal gratification, while Jacob sought God's blessings, and received Isaac's blessing.

But Esau held a grudge against Jacob and vowed to kill him. Jacob had to run for his life. God continued to reveal Himself to Jacob in a vision where He renewed his covenant made with Abraham, firmly passing on the torch:

I am the Lord, the God of your father Abraham and the God of Isaac. I will give you and your descendants the land on which you are lying. Your descendants will be like the dust of the earth, and you will spread out to the west and to the east, to the north and to the south. All peoples on earth will be blessed through you and your offspring. I am with you and will watch over you wherever you go, and I will bring you back to this land. I will not leave you until I have done what I have promised you. (Genesis 28:13-15)

Jacob was awestruck and called the place Bethel because *"Surely the Lord is in this place... This is none other than the house of God; this is the gate of heaven"* (Genesis 28:17). He makes a declaration of faith that Jahweh will be his God (Genesis 28:21).

Following this declaration God starts a process to re-create, refine and transform Jacob, so much so that Jacob becomes one of the big three linked to our understanding of God's identity: we typically refer to God as the God of Abraham, Isaac and Jacob. How does Jacob move from being a dubious character to becoming one of the great patriarchs of Israel, the nation bearing his name? These same two words that God says again and again, sum it up: I will. It is God's will. God has a plan for Jacob, which includes sanctification by sending him to school in the wilderness.

A WALK IN THE WILDERNESS

Jacob is sent to spend twenty years with his uncle Laban, a man as adept at double-dealing and trickery as he is. Jacob sets his sight on Laban's daughter, Rachel, and agrees to work for seven years for her hand in marriage. When the seven years are up, Jacob is due to receive his reward. After the wedding ceremony and first night with his wife, he wakes up in the morning to a nasty shock: Laban has passed off his older daughter, Leah, on the gullible and perhaps rather drunk Jacob. Jacob agrees to work another seven years for Rachel, which he dutifully does. He and Laban constantly haggle for possessions and wages, while his wives are competing with one another as to how many children they can produce, including having more children with maidservant surrogates. Jacob finally has enough and decides to head back home. He hasn't yet learned about transparency and honesty as he packs up and runs off in the night. Laban tracks him down, and they come to an agreement of separation.

What does all this say about God? God is in the redemption and re-creation business. Jacob finds himself working alongside a person of similar design to himself. If we discover someone who rubs us the wrong way, God may have placed that someone in our life as a mirror, to smooth off our rough edges, and as salt to refine us. Ouch. However, we don't have to do this alone. Immanuel is with us every step of the way. Once we accept His invitation, we are born again, baptized into Christ, having died to our old nature, and having been resurrected to new life in the Spirit, through the glory of the Father. We have access to the Holy Spirit who comes alongside us as our counsellor, comforter and teacher, as He continues His work of sanctification, perfection and re-creation of us into the image of Jesus. "*Therefore, if anyone is in Christ, the new creation has come: The old has gone, the new is here!*" (2 Corinthians 5:17)

God clearly states what He expects of us, "*Love the Lord your God with all your heart and with all your soul and with all your mind and with all your strength... Love your neighbor as yourself*" (Mark 12:30-31). God likes someone who is hot, not lukewarm. He likes people who are 110 percent sold out for Him, and those who will do what it takes to win His blessing. He does His best work with men like Jacob or Elisha who asked for a double portion of the Spirit, and women like Esther, who confronted kings in love and Mary of Bethany who sat at the feet of the King of Kings. He gets excited about someone who steps up and steps out, like Nehemiah, or someone who fights for God's honour, like David. God honours anyone who jumps in, boots and all, like Peter, or a person passionate about his convictions, like Paul. God seeks someone who is wholeheartedly devoted, who wants Him first and foremost, and who is willing to walk through fire with Him.

Back to Jacob, who wants to return to the promised land. School is not yet out. He has to learn that the only way back is through Bethel, the house of God where he met with God, and then through Esau, with whom he has to be reconciled. Jacob still thinks he can buy forgiveness with gifts, negotiations, and bargaining (Genesis 32:20). However, before he meets with Esau, God has a further test as part of his transformation.

Jacob has another God encounter at Peniel, this time a wrestling match with an angel. This is a climax of his life struggle, not merely with Esau and Laban, but with God Himself. Again we see Jacob's persistence and perseverance. He says, "*I will not let you go unless you bless me*" (Genesis 32:26). The crippling of his hip is, in essence, the breaking of his will. His strengths are retained but are purged and redirected. Jacob the deceiver has become Israel the Overcomer (Genesis 32:28). Jacob, under the hand of God has been humbled, redeemed and re-created. Now he is able to be reconciled with his brother, and continue to fulfill God's purpose, expressed in the Abrahamic covenant, to birth a great nation. God even redeems his messy relationships and the polygamy which produces his twelve sons. They become the twelve tribes making up the Israelite nation.

We worship the same Heavenly Father who revealed himself as the God of Abraham, Isaac, and Jacob. We give thanks that no one is beyond the grace and reach of God, no matter how bad they are or what they have done. When we truly encounter the living God, in the Person of Jesus our Saviour, we are a new creation, and all the old selfish needs and desires pass away. The old is replaced with a new nature, with a heart, mind, will and spirit now aligned with God's Holy Spirit who comes alongside us and fills us. We are in a process of becoming; every situation and experience works together for good for those of us who love the Lord. We are part of God's purpose of changing us into His likeness and recreating us for His glory.

If we are truly following Jesus, in order to follow in His footsteps, we need to change direction, change our speed at times, either to keep up or so as not to run ahead. "*This is how we know we are in him: Whoever claims to live in Him must live as Jesus did*" (1 John 2:5, 6).

WALKING IN THE FOOTSTEPS OF JESUS

There's a story of a tramp who one day came to the door of a minister. He was unemployed, asking for help with a job. The minister was heavy-hearted but didn't know how to help. The next Sunday, after a beautiful service, the tramp stood and walked to the front of the church. He shared some of his difficulties, asked what it meant to follow Jesus, and then unexpectedly died. The minister was deeply challenged. As he grappled with the question, he started to live each moment with this question, "What would Jesus do?" It changed his life. He shared this question with his church. He challenged everyone to ask the question, "If Jesus were living in my shoes, what would He do?" He asked them to pledge to consider this question for one year. Remarkable things happened. A journalist had to change the way he wrote articles; a singer thought more carefully about the words of the songs she sang; a businessman was challenged to make ethical business decisions. For all, these changes came with a cost that varied from discomfort to professional jeopardy. What situations do we face that demand an answer to the question, what would Jesus do?

In 2005, a tent city began in the park next door to Church of Our Lord. It was a testing time as we had to walk the line between being good neighbours on one hand and being good stewards of our property on the other. There was deep concern that our hard work in beautifying our church was being disrespected by those who defaced, stole and destroyed it. We were faced with the question of what Jesus wanted us to do. He always found time for social outcasts: the beggars, the lepers, the petty criminals, and even the corrupt white-collar tax collectors. He was criticized for associating with such sinners. Who were these new neighbours of ours? Many were idealistic young people, some with no place to live; others were hardline drug users and petty criminals. As we took the time to get to know them personally, we discovered each one had a personal life story, often filled with hurt and hardship. Some were polite, courteous and grateful. Others were abusive, destructive and disrespectful. We had prayed for the Lord to bring us the people to whom He wanted us to minister. Of course we were thinking of all the nice shiny apartments being built around us. What if the Lord sent us seventy-five not-so-lovely or shiny tent people as well? They desperately needed to know the transforming love of Jesus in their lives. We were given a small window of opportunity to share the Gospel. But it came out of relating to them where they were rather than thinking they should be just like us before we got involved. At the same time, we set boundaries in an attempt to protect our property and to ease the fears of our folk. Some started coming to our cafe service. They often helped themselves to coffee and cookies and left. But a few stayed for the whole service and heard the Gospel. God had opened a door into their lives so we could walk with them. A challenging time became a great blessing.

Jesus calls us to follow Him. When He calls, there is no discussion about future prospects, direction or programs. This is not a call to follow an ideology, a philosophy or a policy, but to follow a person. We see this as the disciples responded to Jesus's call by immediately leaving their nets, their source of income, and their families to follow Jesus (Matthew 4:19-22). The calling of Levi is another such instance. One moment he is sitting at his tax table counting money, the next he is he standing up, leaving his table and following Jesus (Luke 5:27-28). The call is simply to follow Him. This is true from our first steps to our last. But in this encounter with some wannabe disciples, we see two possible dangers.

RUNNING AHEAD

The first danger is that of running ahead of God. As Jesus is walking along a road, a man promises him, "*I will follow you wherever you go*" (Luke 9:57). Jesus gives him a reality check when He says, "*The Son of Man has no place to lay his head*" (Luke 9:58). He challenges this overeager enthusiast to understand what he is signing up for. On another occasion, Jesus is teaching His disciples what it means to follow Him and preparing them for what lies ahead (Matthew 16:21-27). Peter offers some advice, but only hears half the story. He immediately jumps in with, "*Never Lord… This shall not happen to you…*"(Matthew 16:22). He doesn't seem to hear the second part about being raised to life. Jesus responds; "*Get behind me, Satan!*"(Matthew 16:23). Impetuous Peter has jumped out of line and is running ahead of Jesus. He is saying come this way, I know best, follow me. How often do we run ahead of Jesus and expect Him to fit into our agenda?

But why does Jesus respond the way He does? The temptation was the same as in the wilderness and Gethsemane—to avoid or bypass the Cross. Jesus immediately prevents Satan from using Peter to sidetrack Him. Peter's best intentions are to save Jesus from suffering, but instead he is promoting the enemy's intention. We want a life with God, and seek it through religious patterns, trying to be good and going to church. We forget the central truth that Jesus died in our place. We are called to follow Him; that means taking up our cross, dying to self and being resurrected as new creatures.

Whoever wants to be my disciple must deny themselves and take up their cross and follow me. For whoever wants to save their life will lose it, but whoever loses their life for me will find it. What good will it be for someone to gain the whole world, yet forfeit their soul? Or what can anyone give in exchange for their soul? (Matthew 16:24-26).

FALLING BEHIND

The second danger is that of falling behind God. Two would-be followers of Jesus wanted to attend to their own business first (Luke 9:59-62). Both sound like legitimate family concerns but Jesus abruptly shuts them down. Why is Jesus so hard on them and what does it tell us about His expectations? "*Lord, first let me go and bury my father*" (Luke 9:59) could mean the man's father had died and he needed to arrange the funeral, but more likely he wanted time to see out his responsibilities to his aging father and wait until he died. Jesus said to him. "*Let the dead bury their own dead, but you go and proclaim the kingdom of God*" (Luke 9:60). Another requests more time to say goodbye to his family (Luke 9:61). Again Jesus is hardline in his response. "*No one who puts a hand to the plow and looks back is fit for the kingdom of God*" (Luke 9:62). They wanted to follow Jesus, but on their own terms and according to their own timetable.

All of us face the same temptation at some time and we all know people who come up with these familiar excuses. The trouble is that we can wait too long and the window of opportunity closes. Jesus expects immediate obedience and submission to His Lordship. When we say, *let me first...*, His answer is that we are first to follow Him and seek his Kingdom. Then everything else follows and falls into place.

Our place is right behind Jesus, following in His footsteps.

TURNING AROUND

When we find ourselves running ahead or falling behind, we need to turn around. This starts with confession: taking responsibility, being honest about what we've done and apologizing to God.

It continues with a decision. We can be endless procrastinators delaying decisions until everything is lined up just right. We have been given the gift of free will and so to get anything done, we make a choice. Whether it is to change a habit or repair a relationship, tidy a room or write a paper, turn around and change direction, it takes a choice.

Decisions are connected to faith. If we don't actually believe anything will be accomplished, it probably won't. To become a Christian requires faith that declares in words what is in our heart. *"If you declare with your mouth, 'Jesus is Lord,' and believe in your heart that God raised Him from the dead, you will be saved"* (Romans 10:9). This is true of many other situations as well. For example, as we learn to see people through the eyes of faith, we come to see them as God sees them, and it makes a huge difference in our attitude towards them. Who are the Jacobs we know? How do we view those close to us? With a change of lens, they are no longer that cranky old husband or wife, indifferent or rebellious teenager, ill-tempered and unfair boss, but God's beloved child who is in the process of being changed into the likeness of Christ. The words we speak will reflect our heart attitude. All these steps are important, but without the last, nothing will actually happen. We have to act.

The Bible is full of action words: come…deny…take up…follow…walk. It is the simple act of doing something that leads to the next step and the next step, and soon we find ourselves walking. Will we be proactive today and walk with Jesus? Are we running ahead, falling behind or following in Jesus's footsteps? What specific pattern of behaviour do we need to change when we ask the question, "What does Jesus call me to do if I am to be more like Him?

One of the great gifts of the Gospel is that no one, not even someone like Jacob, is beyond hope. Everyone has the opportunity to start over as a new creature in Christ.

Questions

How do you feel about God's choice of Jacob over Esau? With whom do you most identify? Can you think of any Jacobs or Esaus in your life? Pray for them.

Read 1 John 2:5-6. How should we walk in the same way Jesus walked? Can you think of any area of your life you would change if you seriously asked, "What would Jesus do?

Read Matthew 16:21-23, and see how Peter tried to run ahead of Jesus. How do you fall into the same trap? Read Luke 9:59-62.

"Let me first..." What does this tell us about Jesus's expectations? Share ways you have said to the Lord, Let me first…

Would you describe yourself as flexible and open to change, or immovable and thinking others need to change?

Read 1 John 1:9. Why is confession the place we have to start to change? Are you a procrastinator, abstainer, or immediately decisive when it comes to decision-making?

In what areas do you need to make changes to get in line and walk with Jesus?

CHAPTER 13

Beginning Anew

Even when we do start out right, we can discover at any stage in life that we have lost our way and have to start over. Generally, this happens as we get older, and our plans go astray. Many have found their life dreams of living happily ever after shattered by divorce or death. Others have been cut from their well-paying jobs and struggle to survive in volatile economic times. Still others discover people with questionable motives have manipulated, stolen and destroyed from them, leaving them with broken dreams and crushed spirits. Once vibrant healthy people have to completely redirect their lives as they cope with debilitating diseases or the results of an accident.

Some people undergoing major change have learned lessons that prepare them for such major change, while for others it is an all-new and steep learning curve.

How can we start anew after dealing with challenges that seem to derail everything? In order to finish, we have to start, keep going, and restart when we get stuck. I draw some principles from my earlier book, *The King of Hearts*.

DAVID THE OVERCOMER

We know where David finished: the king who united Israel. We also know some of his major failings. But where did this man after God's own heart begin? The youngest of Jesse's sons was the shepherd of the family flock, yet the one Samuel recognized as Israel's future king. After a dramatic beginning to his public life, David spent much of his early life avoiding the anger of a jealous King Saul.

WAITING

There is a season and time for everything. Waiting is not passive, but active. David showed up at the big show of the time when Goliath was taunting the Israelite army who trembled in their boots (1 Samuel 17). Too young to be in the army, David was only there on an errand for his father to bring a lunch to his brothers. David was faced with the same situation as everyone else. The difference was they were paralyzed with fear, while he was not.

David showed curiosity, the quality of people who get things done. He started to ask questions because he could not believe that one man could demoralize and immobilize the whole army. Most people are stuck in that kind of thinking, but David was different; he wanted to know why no one was doing anything. Additionally, for a young man with no means, the bounty payment caught his attention. The lesson is that opportunities arise for those who get off the couch, ask the right questions, are prepared to take risks, and be ready for action.

DOING

After finding answers to his questions, David made his move. He rejects the king's offer of the latest high-tech equipment, and settles on using what he know best, his trusty slingshot with five smooth stones. The whole Israelite army had the opportunity to stand up to their nemesis, but no one was prepared to take the risk. David stepped out of his comfort zone to make it happen and demonstrates the simple lesson of the difference between getting the job done or not.

When we are faced with an overwhelming task, we may become paralyzed. Then it is important to do something appropriate to the problem, whether that is prime the pump, make a phone call, write an idea on paper, buy some materials, clean one corner of the room, step out on the playing field, or whatever it takes. The key is breaking the task down into manageable proportions. As they say, "How do you eat an elephant? One bite at a time!"

David took the first step one step by volunteering, followed by the next step of facing Goliath. Each step required another, from aiming his slingshot, to getting closer to his rival, and finally releasing the missile to its target. Of course this is not yet enough. For David, taking on such a gigantic challenge ultimately required more than being prepared for action. His real strength lay in his motivation and faith declaration.

FAITH

Could David have seen the big picture of where all this would propel him? Probably not. But to accomplish anything, we need to have a reason. David's motivation came from his faith in a power much bigger than himself. He could not stand to see the name of His Lord and God dishonoured. He asks in outrage, *"Who is this uncircumcised Philistine that he should defy the armies of the living God?"* (1 Samuel 17:26b). This description of Goliath had less to do with his physical makeup and more to do with circumcision as the sign of God's covenant with His people.

The Israelite army saw the impossibility of the situation while David saw with eyes of faith that all things are possible in and through the God he knew. *"I come against you in the name of the Lord Almighty...for the battle is the Lord's, and He will give all of you into our hands"* (1 Samuel 17:45, 47). David was willing to step up. The pattern of Israel as a nation was full of ups and downs, obedience and disobedience, judgement and forgiveness, failure and starting again. The prophets knew all about these cycles, and constantly challenged Israel to recognize and repent when they failed, but also to rediscover the God who called and loved them.

We leave David for the moment and turn to one such prophet who speaks of starting afresh, something that is key to finishing well.

ISAIAH'S WORD OF RENEWAL

"But now, this is what the Lord says—He who created you, Jacob, He who formed you, Israel: 'Do not fear, for I have redeemed you; I have summoned you by name; you are mine'" (Isaiah 43:1). In this one verse, Isaiah describes the major characteristics of God: Creator, Reformer, Redeemer and Commissioner. As God created and formed the earth, just as He created and formed humanity, so He created and formed Israel the nation. He summoned, called and commissioned them for his special purpose and mission. Throughout Isaiah, we see these purposes being worked out, prefiguring the coming of Messiah, and making His new creation.

Israel sits in captivity in Babylon while her own country is a pile of rubble, a wasteland. Isaiah brings forth God's Word beginning with the signature declaration of God's identity, *"I am the Lord, your Holy One, Israel's Creator, your King"* (Isaiah 43:15). There follows the statement declaring what will come next to be Jahweh's authoritative will: "*This is what the Lord says—He who made a way through the sea, a path through the mighty waters*" (Isaiah 43:16). When the children of Israel had been escaping from Egypt, God had intervened to do the impossible; He made a way through the sea. He reminds them how much more He can do the same again and make a way through captivity to freedom through whatever obstacle stands in the way of His purposes.

Hundreds of years later, Mark brings a similar message of new opportunity, that in the midst of uncertainty, defeat and despair, God will send a messenger ahead of the Messiah (Mark 1:1). Note again the declaration of God's unshakable intention, "I will!" The messenger here is John the Baptist, "*a voice of one calling in the wilderness, 'Prepare the way for the Lord, make straight paths for Him*" (Mark 1:3). He points to Jesus Christ, the Son of God.

"FORGET THE FORMER THINGS, DO NOT DWELL ON THE PAST" (ISAIAH 43:18)

Isaiah encourages Israel not to dwell on her exile, the problems of the past, or the conditions of the present, but to focus on who God is and His will for them.

Similarly, at the time of the coming of Jesus, many missed the new thing God was doing because they were enslaved to the former things of their past. The Roman occupation—with Herod's insecurity, brutal oppression, and pantheon of gods—looked down at the Jewish expectation of a Messiah. Pharisaic traditionalism, legalism and an inability to change blinded Israel's leaders so they missed the very Messiah for whom they were waiting. How about us? The wrong way to look at the past is to get bogged down in its failures or in nostalgia about the good old days. The right way is to "*review the past for me*" (Isaiah 43:26). We are to salvage what we can, honestly face up to our responsibilities, learn from our mistakes, receive God's rebuke and discipline, keep our eyes fixed on Him, and then look to a new start in the future.

"SEE, I AM DOING A NEW THING" (ISAIAH 43:19)

Isaiah offers hope for the future, liberation from Babylonian captivity, and a return to Zion. The question he implicitly poses for us is this: What is God asking us to do new and differently because He is doing a new thing.

Here are two everyday examples. When it comes to worship services, we are all familiar with the tensions, preferences and expectations when it comes to musical choices. Pastors and worship leaders put in a lot of prayerful preparation as they try to balance the favourite and familiar with new songs. The classic hymns are full of great depth and meaning. At the same time, God speaks through the psalmist and prophets of the day in the new songs. It is a case of both/and rather than either/or as we bring to the Lord our fullest expression of worship in the beauty of holiness.

In another context, people make resolutions every new year, hoping for a better life. Most are broken before the end of the month. The reality is that the only way for resolutions to benefit our life is for them to become part of our everyday lifestyle. That includes honesty in facing where we are, clarity in knowing where we want to go, the right choices and changes in action, belief and perseverance. But there is good news on both of these fronts.

We live in the New Covenant era. We are the beneficiaries of all that Jesus Christ, the Son of God has established. The Book of Acts shows the Holy Spirit working in and through the Church. That same work and way continues to this day. At this moment, we stand at a particular date in *anno domini,* the year of our Lord. Each of us are on our journey through the time that has been set before us, between gestation in our mother's womb and the day we are called to heaven. Put your own information and date into the continuum then ponder and consider, Lord, what is Your plan; what do You want for us this day, this year?

We have already seen the difference between *chronos* and *kairos* time in which He is working out His divine purpose. At any time in our year or day, He can create a new beginning, a new relationship, a new opportunity, a new inspiration, a new song, a new thought, a new situation.

The New Testament emphasizes the same principles as Isaiah, the same calling to keep our eyes fixed on Jesus, the Author and Perfecter of our faith. It's all about Jesus, not about us. This is the starting point for our worldview.

"HE WHO MADE A WAY" (ISAIAH 43:16)

As we start each new day and year, can we start afresh with a blank canvas? *"In the last days, God says, I will pour out my Spirit on all people"* (Acts 2:17). I believe we are living in these last days, these Pentecost days now. What is the Spirit saying to us in these days? Can we review the past without dwelling there? What are the former things that God wants us to forget so we don't dwell there? Can we forget the past hurts and problems that drag us down?

As we have seen, the Bible is full of characters just like us, facing similar challenges. Here is someone who was given a second opportunity and who began anew.

JOSEPH—FROM PRISON TO POWER

Are you a dreamer? Have you ever had a promise from God, but then had to wait a long time while dealing with problems and challenges which seem to obstruct its fulfillment? Have you ever felt let down and disappointed, betrayed and abandoned? Have you faced false accusations and injustice? Then you will have much in common and find great comfort in the life of Joseph.

In spite of his many hardships, Joseph was blessed by God and showed his faith and trust throughout his trials. He is another living example of how God works for the good of those who love Him (Romans 8:28). Joseph had a dream which he shared with his brothers. As a naïve and immature seventeen-year-old maybe there was some one-upmanship over his brothers or perhaps he was just excited to share this revelation with them. With ensuing events, I am sure it must have come to feel more like a nightmare. Certainly flaws of human nature in Joseph and in others seemed to conspire against fulfilling the dream God gave him, whether that was the lust of an aristocratic wife, the jealousy of his brothers or the absent mindedness of people who owed Joseph favours, not to mention the aforementioned immaturity in Joseph himself.

I HAVE A DREAM

Do you have a dream? As a young student in South Africa, I remember sitting in my parents' basement listening to a vinyl record of Martin Luther King's famous *I have a dream* speech.

That is one kind of dream, a vision that inspires and touches the heart, which was especially relevant to a young student in apartheid South Africa. This speech inspired me to see through the injustice of our society, to seek the glory of the Lord and His love for each and every person, regardless of the colour of their skin.

God says He will pour out His spirit so that we will see visions and dream dreams (Acts 2:17) but I wonder whether we still expect God to speak to us in supernatural ways. We hear testimonies of how He is supernaturally revealing Himself to people in nations where there is hostility to the Christian message. I also know some of us have had the personal experience of being awakened in the night with a dream from the Lord.

When I came to the Church of Our Lord, I had a visionary kind of dream of seeing the beautiful building with which we had been entrusted, renovated, restored and expanded into a multifunctional centre for ministry and mission. I had a dream to see lives touched with the Gospel of Christ, from the streets to the houses of Parliament, from the homes to the businesses, and to the far corners of the earth.

The fulfillment of this dream required going through ups and downs, facing challenges and disappointments, and partnering with Kingdom-minded people. As a simple pastor, my dream is still very similar, that we who are the Church would embody a faithful witness to the Good News of Jesus Christ. My question is this, "Do we recognize that we are in a marathon not a sprint, from birth to death. As we look back, can we recognize the hand of the Lord working out His purpose?"

FINISHING SCHOOL

Before his dream would be fulfilled, Joseph had to go through a tough training school, preparing him to finish well. He never forgot his roots enabling him to make the most of his circumstances, no matter how difficult.

Born one of the youngest in a tribe of brothers and half-brothers would be difficult enough. Joseph was also the favourite son of his father's favourite wife. (Genesis 37:3). Dad gave him special favour, including the infamous coat of many colours, which did not endear him to his brothers. In fact, *they hated him and could not speak a kind word to him"* (Genesis 37:4). Here we see how such favouritism can wreck family relationships.

Joseph was anointed by God with an incredible gift, a God-given ability to receive and interpret dreams but we can see that no matter how gifted, the messenger is often still a sinful human with feet of clay. Joseph has dreams of sheaves of wheat bowing to him. Even the sun, moon and stars bow to him. He proudly points out that this was all of his brothers bowing to him. Naturally his brothers respond by hating him all the more (Genesis 37:8). This really put a target on his back. However, even though he obviously irritated them, their treatment of him was unimaginable. They plotted to kill him and threw him into an unused water cistern while they decided what to do. Judah showed some mercy, convincing them to sell him into slavery with Ishmaelite traders for twenty shekels of silver. The traders in turn sold him to the captain of the Pharaoh's guard. How frightening for a young boy to be thrown into a dark hole, to be taken by complete strangers to a foreign land, to be separated from his loved ones. I wonder whether his brothers thought through how this would impact him or their father. Jealousy is a powerfully blinding and self-serving destructive force.

Although it may not have seemed so at times, God had Joseph under His tutelage and protection for His long-term purpose. God still patiently worked out His purpose, dealing with human sin and personal flaws.

Wherever Joseph went, blessing, success and prosperity followed. It didn't take long before Joseph was recognized by his boss, Potiphar, and was promoted to chief in the household. However, there were more tests to come, and this time it was at the hand of Potiphar's bored wife who tried to seduce the young and handsome Joseph. Joseph demonstrated his honesty, integrity and trustworthiness by rejecting her advances. In this he showed not only loyalty to his boss, but to his God, while at the same time honouring marriage. You would think he might be rewarded for his trouble. But, as they say, hell hath no fury like a woman scorned, and Potiphar's wife vented her fury by making a false accusation against him. Joseph was unjustly accused, punished and thrown in prison. It is a reminder of how Jesus faced trumped-up charges, as have many God-fearing believers.

Yet once again we see how God's purpose cannot be thwarted. Instead of languishing in self-pity or blaming God, Joseph makes the most of his situation and is recognized for his quality of character: "*The Lord was with Joseph and gave him success in whatever he did*" (Genesis 39:23). Again he is promoted to a position of influence, and is able to use his gift. He interprets dreams for a butler and a baker. Although the butler promises to speak on his behalf, he forgets all about Joseph. The result is two more years of imprisonment. If he had been clogged up with bitterness, anger, and resentment, would he have been able to hear from God? Perhaps not.

During these years of waiting, there must have been times when Joseph wondered if he had been forgotten and abandoned. It would have been easy to complain and wonder why he was wasting away in prison instead of being recognized as the super-star dreamer and interpreter.

What can we learn from Joseph? Do we harbour bitterness in our soul? Are we waiting for vengeance and retribution? Are we caught in some prison of past hurt, abuse, guilt, injustice, abandonment and betrayal? Or are we living in the present, making the most of our situation? Are we waiting until we feel better, see conditions improve, and overcome those obstacles? Could we then discover that time has passed us by and that it may be too late? If Joseph, like the Apostle Paul can continue to serve, to use his gift, and be God's instrument while in prison, can we do the same now, today, whatever the circumstance? What do we regard as the prison holding us back? Maybe we feel unappreciated and languishing somewhere—perhaps in a dead-end job, looking after children, or caring for an ailing family member. Seeing those people through God's eyes can change our view. What better investment can we make than in our children, that family member, serving the people in the office, nursing home, or factory? Whatever we are going through, we know the One who has walked in the fullness of humanity, the One who promises to make all things new.

FINALLY, VINDICATION!

Finally, Joseph's moment comes when Pharaoh is looking for someone to interpret his dream. The butler remembers Joseph who is summoned to appear before Pharaoh. We see that he has learned from his experience, expressing humility and deflecting credit to God. Instead of focusing on himself and his dream, he testifies, "*I cannot do it,…but God will give Pharaoh the answer he desires*" (Genesis 41:16). Pharaoh rewards Joseph who becomes, at thirty years of age, the second most powerful person in Egypt. Not bad for a disenfranchised slave and long-time incarcerated convict.

It is thirteen years from his first dream to this promotion. It may have seemed a lifetime for someone in prison, but God works out His purpose in His perfect time. After all these years, Joseph even gets the opportunity for revenge. The drought he predicted causes his brothers to seek refuge in Egypt where they have to find favour with their long-lost brother. Of course the brothers don't recognize Joseph, but he recognizes them. He gives them a hard time but eventually reveals himself, showing godly character as he grant his brothers forgiveness, mercy, and grace. This leads to reconciliation and a joyful reunion. He repays evil with good, declaring his acceptance of God's sovereign will in all things (Genesis 50:20).

One person who exemplified the same patient, forgiving spirit was Nelson Mandela. Twenty-seven years in prison could have turned him into a bitter, angry man. Instead he demonstrated incredible grace and forgiveness toward those who were responsible for his suffering. He went from prisoner to president of South Africa, and one of the most respected persons in the world.

Joseph's starting point resulted in his ending well as God intended all along. Dead ends became new opportunities. Disappointments turned into God appointments.

Questions

What can we learn from Joseph?

- Joseph was given a dream. He faced suffering with patience and faith, was humbled and refined, and eventually saw its fulfillment. What is your dream?
- Joseph made the most of his situation, no matter how hopeless it seemed at the time. Do you choose to see God's intention for good to accomplish His salvation purpose in all your circumstances? Do you seek to serve at all times?
- Joseph faced a test and chose to honour and obey God's commands rather than take the easy route. Are you faithful in the small things so you're ready in the event of a real test?
- Joseph offered grace and forgiveness to those who had treated him so terribly. Have you received the forgiveness offered to us in Christ? Is there anyone in your past or present you need to forgive?

Is your testimony centred in Jesus Christ or in me-centred bad news?

What is the new thing God is doing and wants to do at this stage of your life? What do you see?

CHAPTER 14

Seeing Is Believing

If you ever feel disappointed in God and wonder why His promises do not seem to live up to expectations, you are not the first and probably not the last. But when we want to develop resilience and turn those disappointments into God appointments, we turn to two heroes of the faith with remarkable similarities, one from the Old and one from the New Testament.

GIDEON'S FLEECE FAITH

Gideon is quietly minding his own business, threshing wheat in a winepress when he comes across an angel sitting under an oak tree on his father's property. The angel delivers a message from God, that God is with Gideon and that Gideon is a mighty warrior (Judges 6:12). Although God affirms Gideon, and specifically calls him, Gideon's response is underwhelming.

PARDON ME, MY LORD

"Pardon me, my lord,…but if the Lord is with us, why has all this happened to us?" (Judges 6:13) I love his very polite, *pardon me, excuse me, sir*. He goes on to raise doubts about God, and then to express doubt in himself.

After forty years in the wilderness, the Israelites had crossed the Jordan River and entered into the promised land, which had been described as land of milk and honey. Perhaps they had expected to drink honey milkshakes and eat lovely bunches of grapes but instead they had faced giants opposition. During Gideon's time alone, six times Israel was under the oppression of other nations, including Mesopotamia, Moab, Ammon, and Philistia. At the time of the angelic visitation, the Midianites had attacked them and the Israelites wondered if the Lord had abandoned them.

Isn't Gideon expressing what we sometime feel? *Pardon me, Lord, we hear about all the wonderful things you did in the past, things you are doing elsewhere. What about us? Have you abandoned us? Where are you, God? Pardon me, Lord, instead of a life of milk and honey, it has been the sweat of my brow paying the bills trying to survive, dealing with illness, children who have turned away, coping with annoying church members who think differently from me, unfulfilled dreams and expectations. Pardon me, Lord, we had such high hopes, yet it has been one struggle, one letdown, one disappointment after another. Pardon me, Lord, if you are with us, why has all this happened to us, why do bad things happen to good people, why can't Christians behave better, why don't we see the same power, miracles, signs and wonders we hear took place in the past, and happen elsewhere? Oh, Lord, where are you?*

As we view Israel's life, in the first verses of Chapter 6, we see a pattern. When Israel sins, they are overpowered by a foreign nation. Then they turn back to God, who sends a prophet or judge to remind them what God has done. They are delivered and are given instruction but they don't listen and instead disobey again, and the same cycle starts up all over.

Church history shows a similar pattern: Things go off the rails, a person or movement starts a reformation or revival which restores a biblical truth that has been lost, they lose track again, and so on. For example, the Reformation recovered truths such as the authority of Scripture, salvation by grace and the priesthood of all believers. Since then much of what was recovered has been lost again to large portions of the Church.

I WILL, YOU WILL

Note that God is the one who acts, the same message given to the other leaders from Abraham to Joshua and throughout the Bible. All God tells the Israelites is not to worship the gods in whose land they are now living (Judges 6:10), but guess what they do?

God chooses Gideon as the instrument of deliverance but Gideon offers his very polite skepticism about his own abilities. Don't we do this all the time? Poor me, I am the smallest, weakest, most unimportant, insignificant…His concerns are similar to Moses's excuses about his inability to lead (Exodus 3, 4).

They also sound similar to my own excuses. As a teenager I was asked to read a lesson in church. I knew exactly my answer, "Not me." God had other ideas and would not let me off the hook. Three months later I stood up in front of church. I was perspiring, my knees were shaking, my lips were trembling, and my glasses slipped down my nose, but I read the lesson. Three months later I preached my first sermon at a youth service. I preached everything I knew in no particular sequence, and after two minutes sat down. But one small step of obedience led to the next step. This is how anyone called by God moves forward.

On the one hand, God wants us to recognize we cannot do things in our own strength. Gideon shows humility but he also falls into the trap of focusing on himself and what he cannot do, rather than on what God has promised to do. God says, I will do it because you cannot; you will do it because I can. When the Lord is with him, Gideon is a mighty warrior.

GIVE ME A SIGN

Now it gets interesting. Gideon is not satisfied with God's word and assurances. He wants a sign that it is really God talking to him (Judges 6:17).

Gideon makes an offering and sees it cooked by divine intervention, with fire from a rock (Judges 6:21).

He may have been a reluctant warrior, but once Gideon gets going, he doesn't play around. Though afraid, he starts his mission by demolishing the Baal altar and cutting down the Ashram pole (Judges 6:28) in direct obedience to the Lord's command. This does not win him any popularity contest with the people of his village. (Note: The altar and pole were on his father's property. We can't vandalize other people's property, but we do need to ensure that our own household is in order. Once I was given astrology information. I stored it in a drawer and forgot about it. One day the Lord reminded me and told me to get rid of it. In prayer I broke any influence or hold it may have had on me, and threw it away.)

Now the mighty warrior is caught up in a battle. The townsfolk want to kill him. The Midianites, Amalakites, and a growing army cross over the Jordan, amass and prepare to attack. Gideon is not alone as he called the people to arms. But once again he needs reassurance, and here we have the famous fleece test. He says to God,

If You will save Israel by my hand as you have promised—look, I will place a wool fleece on the threshing floor. If there is dew only on the fleece and all the ground is dry, then I will know that You will save Israel by my hand, as You said. (Judges 6:36, 37)

God does this for him. Still not satisfied he asks God for another sign, this time in reverse, making the fleece dry while the ground was wet with dew. God comes through again. Gideon comes to a point of belief and is ready to go to battle.

But now it is God who is not satisfied. He wants to trim the troops. All who are afraid are allowed to go back, and twenty-two thousand men leave, while ten thousand remain. But the Lord still feels there are too many, and once again they trims them down, this time to three hundred. In spite of being overwhelmingly outnumbered, with God on their side, they go on to victory.

While we can identify with Gideon's doubts, I urge you to be careful of turning this fleece test into a method of receiving God's guidance. The account about our New Testament Gideon, Thomas, offers a better way forward. Thomas is renowned as the cautious doubter. Like Gideon, he needs reassurance. They both seek a sign, and both end up stepping up and stepping out in faith.

DOUBTING THOMAS?

We have all heard of doubting Thomas, but is this a fair reflection of who he is? Thomas wanders into a meeting where everyone is talking about the appearance of Jesus (John 20:24). He had missed the event. We don't know why. He may have overslept or had a pressing engagement, his wife might have told him he had been spending too much time on all this church stuff. Maybe he just withdrew his presence in disappointment that Jesus had been killed. Perhaps he was scared, so thought he'd just lay low. The disciples don't pick on him for not being present; they simply tell him that they have seen the Lord. But Thomas is not buying it.

He says, *"Unless I see…I will not believe"* (John 20:25). Thomas needed visible, demonstrable proof. On the one hand, asking questions and showing genuine inquisitiveness is a great quality. We are told if we seek, we will find. On the other hand, like Gideon, Thomas is adding extra demands, saying unless God does what he wants and proves Himself to Thomas, he won't believe. We have to discover that God is a lot bigger than our experience, our expectations and our world.

However, if Thomas was a doubter, he was also a seeker. Deep down he is saying that he wants to believe. May the Lord turn our doubts into seeking faith, our disappointments into God appointments. May we be asking what God is saying to us personally and to our church. One thing is certain; the Lord is with us. Jesus says, don't doubt, believe.

I remember trying to text my daughter after the birth of our first granddaughter on one of those old flip phones where I had to click once, twice, or three times for different letters. After an hour all I could get out was the word "baby." Then I got an up-to-date iPhone and texting became very easy. Are we relying on old methods to hear from God, like throwing down a fleece, or casting lots to make choices? Some even try forbidden practices like astrology or consulting psychics.

The interaction between Jesus and Thomas gives us clear directives. The key is the Holy Spirit to whom we have already been introduced. Jesus has prepared the disciples for the coming of the Spirit and after his resurrection, He has breathed on his disciples the same *ruach* breath of God who hovered over the earth in Genesis 1 when He says, "*Receive the Holy Spirit*" (John 20:22). But to Thomas, Jesus says, "*Reach out your hand*" (John 20:27). The Bible is about real people like you and me. Gideon, who was willing to say, pardon me, Lord, is like us. Thomas, who honestly shares his questions and doubts is another. Jesus invites Thomas to reach out and touch. His message to Thomas is to stop doubting and believe. God always invites us to reach out and step out in faith.

Like Gideon, we can find reasons to doubt God. There are those who will always try to generalize a problem in order to shift the focus and justify unbelief. For example, the familiar question about why God allows suffering in the world. It is a legitimate question, but many use it as an excuse. If God allows this, then He is not the sort of God who I can believe in, they say. What we are really saying is, unless He justifies Himself to me, I will not believe. Another excuse is the old, "There are all these gods and different religions, why should we believe in this one?" In our pluralistic, relativistic, tolerant and supposedly inclusive worldview of today, believing in an exclusive God who deals in absolutes and expects obedience to His commands does not sit well. Some say let's change God to fit our expectations and requirements. Let's lower the bar and throw out any reference to anything so antiquated as sin and then we can all be a big happy family. When we do this, we create a god in our own image. We say that unless God changes, I will not believe.

There is the story of a navy ship which suddenly came across a light in the middle of their course. The captain communicated by radio, "This is the captain of a very important ship. We are coming through; please move out the way." The reply came back recommending the ship should please move three degrees to the left. The captain was now really mad and repeated his message.; The reply came back, "This is a lighthouse. If you don't change course, you will be on the rocks." It isn't God who has to change but us.

When we take our eyes off Jesus, the natural result is to revert to our self-centred selves. Then it is so easy to slip into depressive doubt where we allow our personal problems to block our belief in God. We ask why God allows this to happen to us. We say that unless He treats us in the custom to which we deserve, we will not believe. We have to make a choice: to listen to the doubters, naysayers and critical voices or to align ourselves with God's thoughts that build and empower belief.

Jesus says to Thomas, "*Because you have seen me, you have believed; blessed are those who have not seen and yet have believed*" (John 20:29). We start with the level of faith we have, which only needs to be the size of a mustard seed. As we believe, we see the Lord; as we believe, we receive. As we believe and obey, the Lord reveals the next step. As we declare our faith, we open the door for the Holy Spirit to influence and accomplish God's intention. There are times for asking prayer, but there are also times for declaration-of-faith prayer. The difference is our focus. Instead of focusing on our need, we focus on who God is, and specifically who He is in relation to our need. For example, if our need is financial, the focus is on the Lord our Provider and in giving thanks for His provision. If it is for healing, we declare faith in the Lord our Healer and testify to the healing we have known. Our declaration opens the door for the Lord to come in and accomplish His purpose.

Thomas decides and declares his faith at last when he says, "*My Lord and my God*" (John 20:28). As we believe, receive and obey, we move from putting conditions on faith to complete surrender and submission. This is the place of freedom, peace, trust, and victory. May we make this move, receive His peace, and share that peace with others.

In response, join other Christians in praying the following prayer:

We confess, Jesus, that You are our Lord and God. We believe in our heart and confess with our lips that You were raised from the dead and are alive now and forever. We call on Your Name for our salvation, provision, protection, healing, deliverance and rescue. We believe You are bigger than our problems; nothing is impossible for You. Come, Holy Spirit; fill our heart, mind, soul and spirit with new faith and hope.

You can also respond by joining Christians in declaring The Apostle's Creed:

I believe in God, the Father almighty, creator of heaven and earth.

I believe in Jesus Christ, his only Son, our Lord.

He was conceived by the power of the Holy Spirit and born of the Virgin Mary.

He suffered under Pontius Pilate, was crucified, died, and was buried.

He descended to the dead. On the third day He rose again.

He ascended into heaven and is seated at the right hand of the Father.

He will come again to judge the living and the dead.

I believe in the Holy Spirit, the Holy catholic Church, the communion of saints, the forgiveness of sins, the resurrection of the body, and the life everlasting. Amen.

Questions

How do you feel about bringing your questions, complaints and doubts to God?

Have you ever wondered why the promises and descriptions of the miraculous often don't seem to be as evident in your own reality? Do you say, "Pardon me, my Lord?"

In a group setting, share your own experience of these questions: Pardon me, my Lord, why has this happened to me/ us? Pardon me, my Lord, how can I…?

In what ways do you identify with Gideon or with Thomas?

How can we move from "unless I see I will not"…to "I believe?" From "pardon me my Lord"… to "yes, amen, Lord?"

How well do you know the Holy Spirit?

CHAPTER 15

Reading the Signs

How do you feel as you watch the incredible destruction caused by natural disasters such as hurricanes and earthquakes? Do you remember the tsunami of 2004 which wiped out whole villages in Sri Lanka, India, Indonesia and Thailand? New Orleans was flooded in hurricane Katrina the next year. We have seen thousands killed and made homeless in earthquakes, tornadoes, floods and fires. There are suicide bombings, air raid bombings and missile strikes, killings at schools and shopping centres. We have economic meltdowns. Many live in fear about climate change and the environmental emergency facing the next generation.

People are afraid. We ask what in the world is going on. How can we make the most of life with destruction all around us? What should we be doing? Being representative of the Body of Christ, how do we interpret these kinds of events? How do we minister to the hurting who ask where God is...or want to blame Him? Even the elect grow weary and doubt. Jesus said, *"You know how to interpret the appearance of the sky, but you cannot interpret the signs of the times"* (Matthew 16:3).

We began this book in the beginning. To make the most of life we need to be aware of the end of the story. Before we look at the signs of the last times, let me say that I am not going to speculate about dispensationalism or different rapture theories.

When we look at *eschatology*, from the Greek word meaning last, we need to view Scriptures addressing last things through three different lenses. Such Scripture verses simultaneously describe events at the time of writing, refer to events throughout history, and, warn about events in the last days. All three lenses are important.

The context is clear from Genesis to Revelation: we live in the middle of a spiritual battle between good and evil, God and Satan, Christ and the antichrist. God is the creator and initiator who has a definite purpose for his creation. From the initial Creation when God looked on his handiwork and declared it was good, to the destruction of harmony through the Fall, this world is the stage for this battle. Although the antichrist spirit has been evident throughout history, the Bible tells us that he will launch a final onslaught in the last days. While the world is focused on all the beautiful, important people and events, from world leaders at their summits to what the latest celebrity is wearing and who scored the winning goal, these are only a backdrop for God's priorities. God is interested in what His people are doing and how they work out His eternal purpose. We need to ensure we know how to interpret His signs.

Jesus described upheaval in the world as birth pains (Matthew 24:8). The acceleration and increase in intensity and frequency of these pains have significance, whether it is an actual woman in labour or as God is preparing for His Kingdom to come on earth as in heaven. Once a woman is in active labour and the waters have broken, birth is very close and in fact, unstoppable. Earthly labour pains point to the conditions which prepare the world for Jesus's return when His undisputed reign will be established.

The description of the seals in chapter 6 in the book of Revelation uncover some of these hidden signs of labour, and have special relevance today.

THE FIRST SEAL: WHITE HORSE OF CONQUEST

I see this as applying to the wars and rumours of wars proliferating all over the world. Most who are engaged in warfare see themselves as white knights fighting for a just cause. Whether it is wars of the past generations, or the more recent, including the insidious terror wars of today, everyone thinks they are the knight on a white horse, bent on conquest.

SECOND SEAL: THE RED HORSE OF VIOLENCE/CONFLICT

This tells us that there will be new kinds of wars, violence and death. This is one of the most troubling signs. September 11 is marked in America's history and psyche, bringing home the face of evil in a new way. For many, going to war is as inevitable as going to work. It is a way of life. Think of all the wars of just the past few years: in Europe, Africa, the Middle East and more. The nature of warfare has changed dramatically with little regard for such rules as the Geneva Convention. Instead we have extreme torture, rape, and public beheadings. Most of us can't comprehend why young people would blow themselves up for a delusion. Outrage of different kinds invades everyday life in formerly peaceful neighbourhoods all over the world.

For all our so-called advanced civilization, we are puzzled why a father would kill his own family, or why seemingly innocent children would beat another child to death, why a schoolboy would shoot and kill classmates, or why a mother would commit infanticide of her own baby.

We have reflected on the social issues such as the breakdown of the family which can lead to this violence, but this seal indicates there is also a spiritual dimension. *"Its rider was given power to take peace from the earth and to make people kill each other"* (Revelation 6:4).

THIRD SEAL: THE BLACK HORSE OF SCARCITY

Jobs, resources, money and food all seem to be found in diminishing supply. With the increasing disparity between rich and poor, world economies at times seem on the brink of collapse. In some countries, a day's wages (Revelation 6:6) hardly buys a loaf of bread, as is the case in places like Zimbabwe, Sudan, Syria, and Yemen where people are starving.

Refugees all over the world flee conditions in one country seeking a better life in another. When this crowds already limited resources, it creates tensions that flummox the brightest minds. Should countries open borders and welcome the crowds ahead of those who have been patiently waiting in line? Or should walls, actual or figurative, be built to protect inhabitants? Whatever the causes, exploiting the uncertainty, confusion and fear, will be the way that the antichrist asserts his rule. Whoever can gain control over the food supply, financial resources and personal information will have power over humanity.

FOURTH SEAL: THE PALE HORSE OF DEATH

Famine, earthquakes, pestilence, and plagues are all mentioned in Revelation. Scientists are struggling to make sense of the changing weather patterns and climate. Earthquakes, floods, fires, hurricanes, tornadoes and tsunamis have impacted many lives.

At the same time medical experts struggle to deal with an over extended health care system caused by old and new diseases which have mutated into deadly pestilence and plagues. Who would have thought that a disease such as AIDS, unknown a few generations ago, could wreak such havoc on the world population, or that the hospital that is meant to make you well is where you can catch a super bug? The latest Coronavirus is being considered a pandemic by the World Health Organization, already has resulted in deaths in many countries, and impacted world economies with the financial markets plunging.

Whatever the cause, the past few years all point to a dramatic increase in the intensity and frequency of these birth pains. Most are a combination of human-caused and natural disasters, but are infused with a spiritual component.

FIFTH SEAL: INCREASED PERSECUTION AND SUFFERING
"I saw under the altar the souls of those who had been slain because of the Word of God and the testimony they had maintained" (Revelation 6:9). As the antichrist spirit arises, there will be a head-on collision with the spirit of the real Christ. The result will be increased persecution. Today millions of Christians are banned, arrested, persecuted or even killed for their faith; one estimate is two hundred million people in more than sixty countries. Yet the media don't often mention such religious discrimination.

We know this was predicted by the One who was tried on false charges, sentenced, and crucified. His martyrs will give testimony, be clothed in white robes of righteousness, and reign with Christ. We give thanks for the faithful witness of the communion of saints of every age around the world.

AN AGE-OLD CONFLICT
Two of the major religions of the world have a long history and deep roots of conflict. We have already met Abraham who laughed when God told him Sarah would have a child. Actually. Abraham was the father of two sons by two different mothers between whom no love was lost. When Abraham and Sarah took matters into their own hands, Ishmael was born to Sarah's servant Hagar, and was given the promise by God to become a great nation (Genesis 21:18). Isaac, Abraham and Sarah's son would fulfill God's covenant promise. Often the heirs of these promises—Judaism, Islam and Christianity—seem to be forever at loggerheads; short of God's intervention there appears to be no hope for a resolution.

THE FIG TREE

The fig tree is seen as a description of Israel, the nation that came through Jacob's sons who formed the Twelve Tribes of Israel. It is Israel who is given the Promised Land in fulfillment of God's promise to Abraham.

Because of continual disobedience and sin, the nation of Israel was constantly defeated, exiled or under foreign domination, yet God is always faithful to His promises. At the coming of the Messiah, the Christ, the Jews rejected Him because they were expecting a political Saviour, rather than a suffering Messiah. God opened the door to the Gentiles, and a new covenant was instituted based on the completed mission of Jesus Christ. This does not, however, mean that God is finished with His people the Jews; quite the contrary. We are called to pray for the peace of Jerusalem (Psalm 122:6).

How should we as Christians regard Israel today? There are views on either side of the spectrum and a number in between, but one salient question is this: when Jesus inaugurated a New Covenant, did it replace the Old Covenant? Replacement Theology is the view that the Church has completely replaced Israel as the new Israel. While Hebrews does tell us that the New Covenant has replaced the Old, it doesn't nullify God's Old Covenant promises, which are both eternal and still being fulfilled.

God's intention is that Jewish people come to know the Messiah they rejected. The spiritual restoration of Israel is closely related to its physical restoration before she recognizes Jesus as Messiah. A detailed biblical theology of this reality can be found in Zechariah, with this conclusion: "*They will look on me, the one they have pierced and they will mourn for him*" (Zechariah 12:10).

THE TROJAN HORSE

How about the other main nation who descend from Abraham? It is a dilemma for us as Christians to understand how to stand firm in our faith in love, without being uncaring and xenophobic.

A common misconception is the belief that all religions are basically the same, and that all roads lead to the same God. Religions generally are about seeking God and following precepts, commands and directions to find Him. Christianity is about God seeking us, culminating in a personal relationship with Jesus Christ. The Koran contradicts the main tenets of the Christian faith, denying Jesus was crucified on the Cross, let alone was resurrected so it is not the same at all.

I want to draw a distinction between militant Islam as a political and religious ideology and the many moderate Muslims who are interested in living peacefully and sincerely following the religion they have been taught. One of the most startling developments over recent years has been the rise of Islamic fundamentalism. They have a goal to impose an Islamic State on the whole world, with a Trojan horse campaign of infiltration, while launching a holy war against all infidels.

While keeping our eyes open so we are not deceived, we need to treat everyone with respect, grace and love, no matter what their beliefs. God loves them and would have everyone come to salvation in Christ. Many Muslims are coming to know Jesus, by recognizing the grace and forgiveness offered by the Gospel, and by having supernatural encounters with the Lord Himself. Pastor Rick Warren, who was inaccurately and unjustly accused of syncretizing Christianity and Islam into what people referred to as Chrislam, spoke well when he said,

> My life and ministry is built on the truth that Jesus is the only way, and our inerrant Bible is our only true authority...You cannot win your enemies to Christ; only your friends, so we must build bridges of friendship and love to those who believe differently so Jesus can walk across that bridge into their hearts...It is nonsense to believe that you must compromise your beliefs, or water down your convictions in order to love someone, or even just treat them with dignity.[5]

THE MAN OF LAWLESSNESS
While the antichrist spirit has been present throughout history, its influence is growing.

> *Don't let anyone deceive you in any way, for that day will not come until the rebellion occurs and the man of lawlessness is revealed, the man doomed to destruction. He will oppose and exalt himself over everything that is called God or is worshipped, so that he sets himself up in God's temple, proclaiming himself to be God.* (2 Thessalonians 2:3-4)

We have already seen this rebellion and inversion of values where evil is considered good, wrong becomes right, together with increased persecution and suffering. As Jesus warned and promised, *"Everyone will hate you because of me"* (Luke 21:17). But at the same time., Jesus says, *"This gospel of the kingdom will be preached in the whole world as a testimony to all nations, and then the end will come"*

---

[5] Surratt, Geoff. "Does Pastor Rick Warren Endorse Chrislam?" pastors.com. July 22, 2011. https://pastors.com/does-rick-warren-endorse-chrislam/.

(Matthew 24:14). While many Western commentators dismiss the Church and its relevance, in the developing world and southern hemisphere, the Church is growing and expanding at an incredible rate.

What are some of the descriptions and characteristics of the antichrist? Two characteristics stand out, deception (2 Thessalonians 2:3, 9) and lawlessness (2 Thessalonians 2:3).

Satan is an angel of light who is a master of manipulation. Today we see this same deception, distortion and dishonesty in every arena. People still fall for the same lies where darkness masquerades as an angel of light. *"They perish because they refused to love the truth and so be saved. For this reason God sends them a powerful delusion so that they will believe the lie"* (2 Thessalonians 2:10, 11).

Satan rebelled against God and is hellbent on undermining God's authority, order and values. Rooted in pride, this results in self-exaltation, inversion of values, boundary-pushing, no self-control, and no absolutes. We see a complete denial, ignorance and outright disobedience to God's Word, truth and ways through deception and rebellion.

The Roman Emperor Domitian embodied the man of lawlessness in the first century, and there have been many such antichrist figures over the course of history. But in the last days one more evil is coming who will proclaim himself to be God (2 Thessalonians 2:4). There will be a time of great tribulation, and he will take control through all means—politics, economy, media, etc. The Book of Revelation gives much more information on these signs and times but we need to be alert, and recognize what is going on in the world around us.

MADNESS AND MAYHEM

There are many examples of a world gone mad with deception and lawlessness. We see multiple mobs rioting in the streets or individuals venting outrage by stabbing, shooting or blowing up people in the name of their cause. People feel let down and disappointed by politicians, social systems, religious leaders, family and friends. In the workplace, deception and dishonesty seem to be the new normal for ethics. Self-interest rules to get as much as possible no matter what the cost to others. In the media, we have news based on specific agendas, opinion and bias, rather than facts and evidence. Government is meant to be God's instrument to bring order in society, but governments can and do also set themselves above the law, abuse power, and mistreat the people they are called to serve.

Youth are particularly vulnerable to deception. Experts are trying to find answers to the consequences of sex without boundaries or responsibilities, while sheer evil floods the market and infiltrates the communication media with addictive violent video games and pornography available with the easy click of a smartphone. Drugs are enslaving a generation of young people, until the only reason for living is to get the next vape or fix.

Of course, turning to the God who created us is too restrictive, oppressive and silly for many in our enlightened age. From Hollywood-hype to politically correct madness, there is an insidious denigration of the Christian worldview and values. Under its prince of lawlessness, chaos and corruption is followed by unease, insecurity and uncertainty, which is in turn followed by anger, outrage and violence.

All the time, the horror of war is a daily reality. With such a bleak outlook, what hope is there? How are we meant to get by, let alone make the most life? I invite you to consider this prophetic word God gave me:

Truly, Truly I say to you: I am the Lord God who created this universe, including the earth you inhabit. I created each of you in your mother's womb. I have loved you with an everlasting love, revealed my heart and mind, intent and purpose, through my Word, spoken by my messengers, embodied in the One in whom My glory dwells. Let it be known that My message is of grace and mercy, salvation and restoration. But there is no love without truth, no justice without judgment. Evil runs rampant on the earth. You have been deceived to think that your eyes can be opened and you are your own god. You eat of the knowledge of good and evil, and choose what is right and wrong in your own eyes. You take what is not yours, distort, deceive, and destroy, plunder and pillage, violate and kill, all to satisfy your own selfish desires. In your arrogance and ignorance you have cast aside My way, My truth, My commands, and the life I gave you, not as your right, but as My gift. You have broken the vows you made before Me and made a mockery of My gift of marriage, defining it in your own image. You disrespect and dishonor, malign and mock those who whom I am recreating in My image, those who are faithful to Me. You stand on your pedestal of pride, which will be a footstool before My throne. You have made an idol of your self-made constitutions and charters, rules and rights, which you think will provide freedom. The only right is My way of righteousness, the only freedom is the freedom I give you. You are dead in your sins, for all fall short of the holiness required to stand in My presence. What has been hidden under the cover of darkness will be revealed in My light. Every knee will bow and every tongue will confess My Name, the name above every other name. I am the Beginning and the End, Jesus Christ, Lord of Lords and King of Kings. Believe and receive Me as your Saviour, or you will stand before and face Me as your Judge. I know all, see all, and judge all. My kingdom is not of this world, I have prepared a place for you. Repent, turn away from your sin, turn to Me while you still have time. Today is the day of salvation. You will know that I was pierced for your transgressions, I am there to carry your sorrows. Come to me all of you who are troubled and weary, I will give you rest. As I have loved you, love Me, love one another. I offer you life in all fullness, life eternal. Believe in Me, obey Me, follow Me! I am the Lord your God and there is no other

God still speaks to us through his Word and by the Holy Spirit.

TURN AROUND

Jesus's message reflects God's priorities and is the same today as when delivered from His mouth when He told His disciples to turn and follow Him. As we have already seen, this is a first step to following Him, but it is also how we keep prepared and ready. The upheaval in the world is to free people and to draw them to know the Creator behind the Creation. As the props are taken away and our natural and religious worlds are turned upside down, God is seeking to gain our attention. We live in a fallen world where Satan is prince, but God has reached out to us in love.

He gave His only Son so we could enjoy eternal life with Him. Yet, they still would not believe. All these calamities are allowed for the specific purpose of shaking people out of their hard-hearted self-centredness and disobedience to God's word. As Christians, we need to be reminded to turn away from sin, apathy and indifference, and turn again to seeking the Lord with all our heart.

STAND UP

The word stand comes up again and again. Standing includes being alert and on our guard, ready for the attacks of evil. It means standing firm in and on the Word of God, the Word that will never pass away while everything else is transitory. It means standing with courage even when others give up or let us down. It means standing together with Christians around the world who are persecuted for their stance. We are to stand firm in the face of evil because we are on the winning side (2 Thessalonians 2:15).

LIFT UP

As we are worship and daily stand in the presence of God, we see things from His perspective. Church of Our Lord is now surrounded by high-rise buildings in downtown Victoria. From inside the church, it seems big and busy with many activities, but looking down from the top of one of those buildings, it seems small.

Sometimes we are overwhelmed by the magnitude of our problems and struggles. As we see them through God's eyes, they take on a completely different proportion, and become more manageable. Let us allow Jesus to lift us up as we rest in Him, in the assurance He can take care of our present challenge. Trust that He has the future in His hands, including our destiny.

We are also called to lift up others in prayer. We are called to pray for the peace of our city, and our nation. The only real lasting peace comes through the Cross, through the Prince of Peace.

Thanks to the vision of a pastor colleague, 1 Timothy 2: 1-8 came to life as a call to *"lift up holy hands in prayer."*

Recently, I have been part of a group of retired pastors who meet and lift our hands to pray for those in authority in Canada. None of us regard ourselves as intercessors, but we all know to listen and obey when God calls. Our intent is not to bring judgment or our own partisan agenda; we simply come to pray. We enter into spiritual warfare against the powers of darkness that seek to deceive and destroy. We come to reclaim the Christian heritage of our nation. Our intent is through prayer to create a spiritual umbrella that covers a whole nation and protects and enables the church to take her rightful place in this nation we call Canada. We pray for the Dominion of Canada to be under the Lordship of Jesus Christ, from sea to sea—from the Atlantic to the Pacific, from Nova Scotia and Newfoundland to British Columbia. We pray we might bless and be a blessing. We pray for people to come to know God our Saviour.

LOOK OUT

Jesus rebuked people for knowing the signs of the weather, but not recognizing the signs of the times. We need to ensure that we are aware of events in the world, but that we filter this through eyes that are finely tuned by the Word of God. We are warned to be prepared and ready.

The disciples ask Jesus the burning issue of the day, whether He was going to restore the Kingdom to Israel. This was the disciples' agenda but Jesus's answer was that,

> *It is not for you to know the times or dates...But you will receive power when the Holy Spirit comes on you; and you will be my witnesses in Jerusalem, and in all Judea and Samaria, and to the ends of the earth.* (Acts 1:6-8)

This is what we should be doing as we await His return.

Jesus said, *"My Father's house has many rooms...I am going there to prepare a place for you"* (John 14:2). To get there, death is the final obstacle, the final test. As Jesus hangs on a Cross, dying, his words show us how to live, and how to die.

Questions

When you look around the world with all its disasters, natural and manmade, what do you see? How do you explain them to unbelievers?

How do you protect yourself from being deceived, given that the nature of deception is that we are unaware of it?

In a world where lawlessness is rampant, how do we walk the line between submission to authority, becoming legalistic, and being free in the Spirit?

Do you have an emergency kit ready in the case of a disaster? How about being ready when the antichrist shows his true colours? How are you prepared?

If the Lord were to return today, would you, would the Church recognize Him? Remember the spiritual leaders didn't recognize Jesus. What are you doing to be ready for the Lord's return? If you are in a group, discuss.

CHAPTER 16

It Is Finished!

Have you ever had the experience of being involved in a project that seemed almost impossible, and then finally getting to the end when it is completed? There's a sense of accomplishment, fulfillment and triumph. I remember those feelings after graduation, a sporting match, the completion of building projects, and more. But when Jesus is at the end of His commission, He isn't taking the victory lap we might envisage. Instead He hangs on a cross like a common criminal, mocked and beaten, seemingly defeated.

Yet in all the uncertainty, inconsistency and complexity of life, the Cross stands at the centre of God's interaction with and purpose for this world. The crucifixion is the most significant event in history, which affects the whole universe and every human being. In the eyes of the world, the Cross is foolishness (1 Corinthians 1:18). But the foolishness of God is wiser than all the wisdom of the world (1 Corinthians 1:25). While we are constantly bombarded with ideas and language, a few words from a dying Jesus, so simple yet profound, stand out with timeless impact two thousand years after they were spoken.

The seven sayings of Jesus on the cross can represent different stages of life and can be an example of how to live and how to die. The way we live is often a mirror of the way we die, and vice versa. As I have said, aging brings out what is inside us—our hopes and our fears, our joys and our sorrows, our contentment and our frustration, even our forgiveness and our guilt.

As we look at Jesus on the Cross, we can see ourselves as God sees us.

THE WORD OF FORGIVENESS:

"Father, forgive them, for they do not know what they are doing" (Luke 23:34).

Jesus is living out what He has taught, offering forgiveness, even to those responsible for His death. Forgiveness is at the heart of God's salvation plan. Jesus forgives the religious leaders who are threatened and exposed, who thought they were doing God's will by getting rid of this troublemaker. He forgives the Roman authorities filled with their own sense of self-importance, the political leaders strutting across the stage, the soldiers carrying out their orders, the people looking on, perhaps with puzzlement or apprehension, like sheep without a shepherd. He forgives all of us.

Where would we have stood on the day Jesus died? Would we have been scattered and in hiding with the disciples, in denial like Peter with all the bravado now burst, hanging around the edges looking on from a distance, standing at the foot of the cross with John, Mary and the one or two? Where are we now?

Can we pray for the ones who have hurt us, asking the Father to forgive them?

THE WORD OF SALVATION:

"Truly I tell you, today you will be with me in paradise" (Luke 23:43).

What does Jesus mean by paradise? Why did one thief get a personal invitation and another not? Why should God let us into His paradise? What significance is the relationship between today and eternity? How can we make the most of today?

Jesus hangs on the cross, with two convicted thieves on either side of him. Instead of thinking of His own humiliation and suffering, He reaches out to them. They have two different reactions: the one mocks and thinks of his own self-interest while the other rebukes his fellow thief, and humbly asks Jesus to remember him when He came into His Kingdom (Luke 23:42).

How aware are we of the people and the needs around us, even in the most trying circumstance?

Can we pray, Lord, remember me? Lord what do you think of me? Am I one of your inner circle of disciples? Lord, forgive me...what am I doing that is not pleasing to you? Lord, receive me. Lord, use me. Where am I running around needlessly? Lord remember me!

THE WORD OF AFFECTION:

"Woman, here is your son...here is your mother" (John 19:26, 27).

As we face death, most of us think of our loved ones. Few show regret for work and business dealings, while most wish they had spent more time with family. From the Cross, Jesus takes care of His natural responsibilities. There were no social assistance programs, no pension plans, and no Joseph around as a provider. Jesus ensures His mother is cared for by a trusted disciple. We recognize that in life and death, love for family is the highest human priority. How is our relationship with those closest to us now?

THE WORD OF ANGUISH:

"My God, my God, why have You forsaken me?" (Matthew 27:46)

How could God's Son feel cut off from His Father? On the one hand, we see Jesus in His full humanity experiencing the darkness of desolation and doubt. He has faced physical abuse, humiliation and embarrassment in front of His followers, loved ones and enemies, as well as rejection by His own. At the same time, in His divinity as the sacrificial lamb, He is bearing the full weight of sin and evil. The consequence is that He is cut off from God the Father, who in His perfection and holiness cannot be present with that sin. In this moment, Jesus feels pain, rejection and separation, but still communicates with His Father from the depths of His soul.

Have we ever felt forsaken by God? How about being forsaken, rejected, let down, abandoned, deserted, betrayed, mistreated by someone? How do we deal with disappointment and despair? It is okay to be honest with the Lord in prayer; He knows anyway. Take courage; Jesus knows and understands.

THE WORD OF SUFFERING:

"I am thirsty" (John 19:28).

Jesus, fully human, experiences the full effects of the human condition and is not exempt from real physical and spiritual pain and suffering. After a long night of terrible treatment, He was weary and thirsty. From the testing in the wilderness through to this moment, Jesus has been tempted in every way we have. All of us have felt the limitations of living in a human body, especially as we start to feel the effects of aging. Tell God, "I thirst!"

More importantly, remember where you can have your thirst quenched. Jeremiah warns, *"My people have…forsaken me, the spring of living water, and they have dug their own cisterns, broken cisterns that that cannot hold water"* (Jeremiah 2:13). What are the cisterns we go to again and again even though they come up empty. Jesus, the fountain of life, says, *"Let anyone who is thirsty come to me and drink. Whoever believes in me, as Scripture has said, rivers of living water will flow from within them"* (John 7:37, 38). By this He means the Holy Spirit.

THE WORD OF VICTORY:

"It is finished" (John 19:30)

What was Jesus expressing in this statement? How could He feel any fulfillment having His life cut short after a short time of ministry? Did He really believe everything He came for was done, over, finished? Was He expressing frustration and defeat? That doesn't make any sense. Jesus knew exactly what His mission was. He had had three years of ministry with three primary areas of focus:

1. *Kingdom intervention*: Preaching, healing and deliverance, which heralded God's intervention in and reclamation of this world and the establishment of His Kingdom.
2. *Discipleship investment*: He invested his life into His apostles, and then more disciples, training them to continue His mission.
3. *Salvation atonement*: All this led to His sacrificial atonement for the sins of the world, offering God's plan of salvation and the gift of eternal life.

Now His earthly mission is complete. He has laid the foundations, done the work, and cries out, *"It is finished."* This is not a cry of defeat, but a declaration of completion and fulfillment, victory and triumph.

Do we know our call and commission? God has a purpose for each of us and we need to know what it is. Then we'll know what tasks to answer with yes or no, know when a task is finished so we won't prolong what should stop, know when to work and when to rest. In this way we prevent burnout, bailing out, group pressure or personal escapism. Until we draw our last breath, we still have time. What needs doing now to get the job done so that when our life is finished, we can say, it is finished, and know we have completed our commission.

THE WORD OF CONTENTMENT:

"Father, into Your hands, I commit my spirit" (Luke 23:46).

Jesus was in complete control as He committed Himself into His Father's care. In this moment, He shows the same close relationship with His heavenly Father as He had lived all His life. He was in a place of peace and contentment, intimacy and openness, dependence and trust, submission and obedience. This was the same in life and death.

In Christ, we daily walk in intimacy with Him through the Holy Spirit in us. It involves submission and surrender of our will to the one we know as Lord of our lives. As we commit to Him in life, so we commit to Him in death. The way we learn our dependence and trust in Him in the small things will determine how we act in the bigger tests. Are we prepared for the final exam? What is the relationship between how we live, how we age, and how we die?

Most of us want to live in peace and security. True peace and well-being come from knowing God's perfect will for our lives. Jesus is the same yesterday, today and tomorrow. This means coming to terms with our failures, hurts, and disappointments. Sometimes we can draw the line and move on, while other times we need help and healing. We learn to live in and make the most of the moment. People obsess over the future, conferring with occult practices such as astrology and other such counterfeits We don't need them when we know the One who says He is the beginning and the end. Following Jesus means submitting, committing and surrendering ourselves wholeheartedly into God's loving hands.

We can pray today, "Father, into your hands I commit my spirit. Father, into your hands I commit my needs, my worries, my family, my finances, my life, my everything. When the time comes to give up my spirit, may I be able to say, it is finished.

It is finished. Jesus' earthly mission is complete. The Word became flesh and dwelt amongst us for a while so we might behold His glory. He called, taught, discipled and sent. He gave His life so we could receive ours. On the Cross, He triumphed over sin, the world, the devil, and death. He was resurrected so we could spend eternity with Him. His work on earth is finished, but His work in heaven, including the leading of His Church is still very much in progress.

It is finished, yet it has just begun. In the end, there is a new beginning as we face our future. This is personal for those of us who are still alive on earth. We have resurrection, an eternal home and a future hope to look forward to. Everything is centred in the Eternal One who is the First and Last, the Light and Life, the One who bears the name above every other name, the Lord Jesus Christ.

Questions

Do we need to be forgiven? For what? Do we need to offer forgiveness? To whom and for what? Can we pray, Father forgive them?

When your time is up, do you know that today you will be with Jesus in paradise? How do you know?

Are you at peace with your loved ones? Is there any unfinished business?

Do you have any unresolved forsaken feelings towards God? What do you need to say to Him?

How thirsty are you? Have you taken up Jesus's invitation to come to Him? How well do you know the Holy Spirit? Are you empty, half-full or overflowing in the Spirit?

What would you like to say at the end of your life? What areas of your life are still unfinished? What needs doing now to get there? What would you like your epitaph to read?

What does peace mean for you? When is it good to struggle, fight, persevere and overcome? When do we need to reach a place of acceptance, dependence and surrender? What is the relationship between how we live, how we age, and how we die?

CHAPTER 17

Facing Our Future

Most of us have questions, concerns and even fears about the future, especially after death. Our limitations in this finite fallen universe make heaven difficult to grasp. As we have seen, God's intervention and incarnation in Jesus Christ gives us enough information for insight into His purpose here and now. We also have been given a tantalizing glimpse of the future. For those who have understood that God's Word provides revelation truth, including how the story ends, we have reassurance and hope. Let's look at how we face this future.

The song "Homeward Bound" by Simon and Garfunkel speaks to all of us who have travelled, through its images of sitting in railway stations wishing for a ticket home. I remember my wandering days. After living by my wits on a hitchhiking trip, coming home was such an incredible comfort. There was a hot meal, shower and warm bed. I was loved, provided for, and secure. My parents made my childhood home a place of security for many years. At our home in Cape Town, and later in Victoria, we tried to provide the same for our own children.

But these places are no longer home. In fact, on a visit to South Africa a few years ago, those familiar houses did not feel like home at all. We had moved on to a new home. Almost all of us have had to move accommodation at some time in our lives. Generally such relocation and renovation involves upheaval and turmoil, not to mention hard work to make the new place into a home. Lynne and I enjoy watching renovation shows on television. The experts show their incredible skill in knowing how to move and rebuild walls, find just the right colour coordination, to turn an old rundown house into a new home. Whatever kind of accommodation we have, coming home is a wonderful experience. But everything associated with this life is temporal and temporary. It all points to a deeper spiritual reality. Our journey through this life is heading for an eternal destiny; we are homeward bound.

A NEW HOME

As we enter into middle and senior years, the choice of where to live becomes more acute. I have seen folk refusing to move out of their large family homes as they rattle around, clinging to rooms filled with furniture, memories, and lots of stuff that eventually someone else will have to discard. Others decide to downsize into a more manageable home. Either way the day comes when decisions have to be made as to whether Mom or Dad can stay where they are or have to move in with one of the children or into a care facility.

My father took the bold step of leaving his home country and his close-knit family. Together with my mother and her mother, he relocated to Canada to be closer to my sister and her family who had settled there. He was in his late eighties at the time, while my mother was much younger at seventy and my grandmother a spritely ninety-eight. This geriatric contingent emigrated to start a new life in their new country. I remember when my brother and I gathered with all of them at my sister's family home in Abbotsford, British Columbia. We sat around the living room, enjoying memories together, but also talking about real life-and-death issues. My father was full of questions about life after death. We were able to break bread and pray. A few months later, at age 89, he died and got to find answers to his questions firsthand. My grandmother received her letter from the Queen before passing away aged 102. My mother was in good health and helped out at my sister's home until the creeping scourge of Alzheimer's began to take hold. Soon it became too much, and after an incident when she was found wandering down the road looking for a game of tennis, we agreed she needed more expert care. She moved into a wonderful Christian care home and was happy there. I had the privilege of praying with my mother at her death. My siblings and I were part of the planning and preparation for both our parents on their homeward journey.

Like moving house, the time before death is not an easy time. It is a time of transition. Our bodies provide the home where our souls live throughout our lives (Psalm 90:10). The uncertainty surrounding death and our closing days in this life can be scary, but it is not the end of the story.

Jesus prepares His disciples for His own death, and their destiny. He says of heaven, "*I am going there to prepare a place for you*" (John 14:2). Jesus was put to death on a cross but three days later, He was resurrected. This is the basis of the Gospel, the Good News that "*Death has been swallowed up in victory. Where, O death, is your victory? Where O death is your sting?...But thanks be to God! He gives us the victory through our Lord Jesus Christ*" (1 Corinthians 15:54, 55, 57).

When Mary finds the grave empty, she does not recognize Jesus because He was in the process of being transformed into His resurrected state. This is the promise given to each of us who confess with our lips and believe in our hearts that Jesus is risen from the dead. Paul writes:

When you sow, you do not plant the body that it will be, but just a seed...so it will be with the resurrection of the dead. The body that is sown is perishable, it is raised imperishable; it is sown in dishonor, it is raised in glory; it is sown in it is sown in weakness, it is raised in power; it is sown a natural body, it is raised a spiritual body" (1 Corinthians 15:36, 42-44).

From the time we are born, we are caught in the process of decay leading to death. The physical weaknesses with which we all struggle will one day be no more as we enjoy our new spiritual bodies raised in power. You can read about the various ways that Paul makes this point. Our bodies are simply the seed, the first step towards our eternal destiny.

With this understanding, there are two more issues that have life-and-death consequences that completely miss God's purpose, and that Paul would describe as foolishness.

The first is a pre-occupation with physical existence. It is foolish not to recognize how all the different kinds of seeds, which represent our physical life, will grow into the splendor of something much more. I have already talked about the importance of taking care of ourselves, but the hedonistic preoccupation with the seed life at the expense of the after-seed life is utter foolishness. Flesh and blood cannot inherit the Kingdom of God, because the perishable cannot inherit the imperishable. This is why we need to be born again. Then God makes His home in and among us (Revelation 21:3).

This is the highest calling in the universe. It begins when we are born of the spirit and continues when we go to our eternal home. Think of the amount of time, effort and money spent on the tasks of maintaining our bodies and earthly life. Now think in comparison how much time is spent on our spiritual development and relationship with the Lord, which has eternal implications.

The second issue concerns another of those difficult ethical matters. We looked at the pro-choice pro-life debate in relation to the beginning of life, but now we touch on this as it impacts the end of life. While none of us can really appreciate the suffering nor the tolerance level of anyone faced with a debilitating or terminal disease, how are we to view assisted suicide? This is now being promoted as a human right by those using the same arguments as are used for abortion.

Again, the starting point determines the outcome. If we start with, *"In the beginning, God,"* we recognize that God is the author of life and death. We also know that this body is in a process of decay leading towards death. To pre-empt that natural process and usurp God's role has ramifications for our eternal destiny, especially if we recognize we are more than a body, that we have a soul and spirit.

If our starting point is self where the focus is on *my* suffering, *my* needs, *my* discomfort, then one can make the arguments that this physical existence is too much to bear, that there is no quality of life. Then we can ask: what is the point? why not end it?

Once again this starting point exalts our choice above God's. It rejects His gift of life to us and ignores His promises for our future. Instead of finding purpose in every circumstance, it allows circumstance to dictate our defeat. In contrast, many have endured physical suffering, while exuding an inner spiritual joy and peace beyond comprehension. I think of the examples already given, such as Joni Erikson Tada and Nick Vujicic, as well as the wonderful saints who have ended up ministering to their family and friends while facing suffering and death. For those whose trust is in God and His promised gift of eternal life, the starting point is *"in the beginning God,"* and the conclusion is, *"in the end, God."* Matters of life and death are His purview and responsibility, not ours!

The human qualities of those who endure and overcome against all odds can inspire everyone never to give up. I love watching triathlon, which test human endurance. I also love seeing athletes who participate together with severely handicapped family members. Their joy and love of life supercede the tragedies and challenges they have had to overcome. They can serve as an inspiration to anyone who is tempted to prematurely end their life, encouraging them to instead leave nature to take its course while they seek the God who created and loves them.

Jesus is the key to this eternal life. Christ has been raised from the dead, the last Adam, the one who has conquered sin and death. God gives us the victory through our Lord Jesus Christ. He offers us the gift of eternal life when we shall be changed, transformed into His likeness. This is His purpose and priority for us. He is going to prepare a place for us. The Gospel truth is that it is only through Jesus that we enter heaven.

A NEW PLACE

As they say in the real estate market, it is all about location, location, location. I have had the privilege of living in some beautiful cities in the world, from Durban and Cape Town in South Africa, to Nottingham in the UK, to beautiful Victoria, BC, Canada.

Canada is usually rated by the United Nations in the top three best countries in the world in which to live (although we also boast one of the highest rates of depression, divorce, suicide, and drugs. Canada has also seen a spike in the use of deadly opioid drugs and the legalization of marijuana, along with other social problems as well.) There is no perfect place on earth, but there is a perfect heaven.

Eternity means that this new heaven is already in existence. Scripture seeks to give us some sense of heaven so we have enough information to say this is where we should want to go, and how to get there. Apocalyptic writing, such as the book of Revelation, attempts to describe the indescribable. John describes what he saw in the Spirit through an open door to heaven. Heaven is full of incredible beauty and power, representatives of the Old and New Covenant Elders, the Church, and the whole of Creation, all bowing in worship before the Lord God Almighty on His throne. Jesus is the groom, waiting for His Bride, the Church.

Here is my personal vision. I was driving down the highway and began to wonder what Jesus was doing right now, in His heaven. When Mary encounters the risen Jesus, he says to her, "I am ascending to my Father" (John 20:17). He was returning to another reality. Sci-fi writers sometimes get close to the truth in their speculations, but miss out because they exclude God. This isn't something I can verify but it is far more believable than speculation such as about life on other planets and UFO's. I believe that there is life in a different dimension beyond space and time, probably the third heaven (2 Corinthians 12:2) to which Paul describes having been transported. Imagine a parallel universe existing alongside this one, a similar world, but perfect, uncorrupted by sin, decay and death. "There will be no more death or mourning or crying or pain, for the old order of things has passed away" (Revelations 21:4). While we are at it, no more lawns to mow, gutters to clean, sewage systems, strata council meetings. No more arthritis, memory loss, tooth-ache. No more misunderstanding, mis-communication, mistakes, mishaps. This is not the new world order of which politicians speak, where political correctness forbids reference to the focal point. In fact, that would be the counterfeit of which much more could be said.

This new world order is centred in heaven, a kingdom so vast it is beyond comprehension with our finite minds. I believe it is teaming with life, including the faithful saints who have gone before us and perhaps other forms of creation unknown to us. I don't see us sitting around on clouds playing harps, or even as I would prefer, sitting under a palm tree sipping mango smoothies next to an infinity pool overlooking the ocean. Instead, I think each of us will be given responsibilities in this Kingdom, which will be similar to but different from the world we know. In fact, this planet is like a prototype of the kingdom. Perhaps there will be something like nations or jurisdictions over which we will have responsible oversight. Ruling all this from the heavenly throne room, is Jesus in His full majestic splendor and majesty. Lord of time and space, earth and heaven, He is the Alpha and Omega, the Beginning and the End, the First and the Last.

Looking forward to such a vision should give us a focus for our homeward journey.

A NEW FOCUS

Rick Warren wrote in one of his letters to pastors all over the world,

> In order to keep us from becoming too attached to earth, God allows us to feel a significant amount of discontent and dissatisfaction in life— longings that will never be fulfilled on this side of eternity. We're not completely happy here because we're not supposed to be! It's not our final home; we were created for something much better...The most damaging aspect of contemporary living is short-term thinking. God calls us to keep the vision of eternity continually in our sights. There is far more to life than just here and now![6]

---

[6] Warren, Rick. *The Purpose Driven Life*. USA: Zondervan, 2002. 5.

For some, attachment to the here and now is strong, and they say let's eat and drink, for tomorrow we die (1 Corinthians 15:32). Paul would call them foolish. Compared with eternity, life is extremely brief. We won't be here long, so we shouldn't get too attached to what we see here. All of us will spend far more time on the other side of death than we will in this earthly existence. When we have an eternal picture, it changes the way we live, and our values need appropriate adjustment. This life is a temporary assignment. School-day memories become more and more distant the older we get. School is not an end in itself, but a preparation for life. Likewise, this existence is a preparation for eternity, an opportunity to become more like Christ. Some are more prepared to go to work, on vacation, or even to the grocery store than they are for this journey that all of us will take. When it is our time to leave this body and this world, Jesus has prepared the way for us to move into our new home.

In the meanwhile, our responsibility is to make the best dwelling for God to make His home. He says, "*Here I am! I stand at the door and knock. If anyone hears my voice and opens the door, I will come in and eat with that person, and they with me*" (Revelation 3:20). Jesus is the guest who is also the host. He is the architect, builder, foundation, interior designer and realtor all rolled into one. Invite Him to design and build the home where He has chosen to take up residence. We are His disciples, being disciplined, corrected, tested, admonished, re-created, and transformed. As His light shines, especially into those darker corners, we are being transformed into His image. This means being true in thought, word and deed. Those who refuse to hear His voice and open their hearts will not enjoy the pleasure of His company. Those who do hear and invite Jesus to come and eat with them, those who sacrifice and lose their life for Jesus's sake will enjoy true fellowship at His table.

We would all love to hear our Master say, "*Well done, good and faithful servant!*" (Matthew 25:21) May we use the resources we have been given to fulfill God's commission so that we may finish well and receive His commendation. While we wait, Paul encourages: "*Therefore...stand firm. Let nothing move you. Always give yourselves fully to the work of the Lord, because you know that your labor in the Lord is not in vain*" (1 Corinthians 15:58).

Questions

What is our picture of heaven? Why should God let us in?

Do you feel the discontentment that Rick Warren describes? Why or why not? How tied to this world are you?

How much time do we spend on the perishable aspects of our life? How much on the imperishable?

How do you feel about dying? Share any concerns and fears, hopes and expectations.

As we remember those times of moving house, think of the upheaval, and then the sense of belonging when we settle. How does this help in facing our transition from this life to the next?

If finishing well is your goal, what do you need to do now to complete what you have started, and what the Lord has commissioned you to do?

CHAPTER 18
In the End, a New Beginning

A s we read the signs of the times, the present and future could look rather bleak. Evil seems to run riot while Christian truth and values, not to mention God's people, are trampled. But God is light, and light always reveals what is hidden. Instead of burying our heads in the sand or collapsing in anxiety and fear, we can open our eyes in the light of God's Word, stand and lift up our heads to see that toward which the signs are pointing.

THE PAROUSIA

The Greek word *parousia,* which literally means presence or coming, refers to the second coming of Christ. There are many schools of eschatology, or theology of the end times, leading to Jesus' return. As that discussion would take a whole book in itself, I am going to keep things simple. We know that God has been actively involved in His creation from Genesis through the call and journey of Israel in the Old Testament, to the coming of Jesus Christ and establishment of His Church. His primary focus has been His Kingdom, which has already come, is still in process, and is yet to be completed. The time when this will be accomplished is at the *parousia.* "'Look, He is coming with the clouds,' and 'every eye shall see Him, even those who pierced Him'; and all peoples on earth 'will mourn *because of Him.' So shall it be! Amen!"* (Revelation 1:7). Jesus is coming again. That is a fact of which we can be certain.

As I sit on our deck, I often look up at the changing cloud formations in the sky and wonder what it will be like when Jesus returns. Will the faithful who are still alive on earth be raised to meet all those who have gone before, a great celebration of heavenly celestial beings surrounding the Son? What will He look like? When Jesus came to this earth, the most religious people didn't recognize Him. When He returns as Lord, will we recognize Him? What is our expectation? I have an image of Jesus with a strong face, kind but piercing eyes but what will He look like when he comes in all His heavenly splendor? Just as we are told to look around and see the signs in this earthly world, we are also told to look up and see what is going on in the heavenly realm. Luke concludes his description of the signs in the heavens and on the earth, with this exhortation: *"When these things begin to take place, stand and lift up your heads, because your redemption is drawing near"* (Luke 21:28).

Look up, for all the signs point to this climax: *"At that time they will see the Son of Man coming in a cloud, with power and great glory"* (Luke 21:27). The same power that raised Jesus from the dead will be manifest in full glory. There will no longer be the waiting for vindication; there will be consummation and fulfillment. The constant battle between good and evil will be over, as the goodness and victory of the Lord Jesus will be clear for all to see. There will be no mistaking His coming, and it will be visible from east to west, like a lightning bolt. All the nations of the earth will then know that Jesus Christ is Lord and King. All the elect will be gathered together in one huge celebration, a party in heaven.

In Canada we are part of the British Commonwealth and the Queen of England is our head of state. Some love all the pageantry and decorum of royalty and would welcome an invitation to a special banquet at Buckingham Palace. Those who do attend such functions dress up accordingly, follow the correct protocol, and generally afford her the respect and dignity of her office. How much more in awe will we be when we come into the majestic presence of the Lord of Lords and King of Kings in all His splendor. Our present Queen acknowledges and understands this greater authority but whether the rulers of the earth recognize Him or not, all power in heaven and earth is in His hands, and they will eventually bow to and confess Him as King (Philippians 2:9-11). Jesus said His Kingdom was not of this world. This Kingdom is God's priority rather than a world that is decaying and perishing. While here on earth, Jesus demonstrated his kingly rule over sin and its consequences. He ruled over nature. He over-ruled disease. He ruled humanity by dealing with the root of our human condition and cause of unrest, sin. He ruled over resources as the Lord who provides for our very need.

We can be grateful and encouraged by the fact that Jesus defeated Satan on the Cross. Jesus, Son of Man, Word become flesh, crucified, dead and buried is the risen ascended Christ Messiah, Lord and King ruling from His heavenly throne. He is truly the One who rules and governs as Almighty God, King and Ruler, and so instead of chaos and upheaval, there will be orderly government and authority. Isaiah calls Him Wonderful Counselor; instead of control and manipulation, there will be counsel, comfort and peace. He calls Him Everlasting Father, the One who provides fatherly stability, provision and care. He is the Prince of Peace. Instead of conflict, violence and division there will be peace, harmony and unity.

This is God's perfect heavenly rule in which we are invited to participate. As we celebrate Holy Communion together, we do so in remembrance of Jesus's death and resurrection, and in proclamation and anticipation of His return. We who are the Bride of Christ will join Him at His heavenly banquet. That is worth all the struggles and waiting, as it will be a celebration greater than we have ever experienced, and to which we can look forward with joyful expectation. We will see and meet the complete and perfect, risen and ascended, honoured and glorified Jesus Christ.

This is the promise for the future. Meanwhile, how we finish our lives determines how we will be received into eternity. And, how we finish is determined by whether we are making the most of every day, every opportunity, to start right, start afresh, and enjoy the abundant life the Lord Jesus offers us. As we age physically and begin that trajectory of diminishment, do we continue to embrace this stage of life as part of God's plan for us? The Lord Jesus invites us to exercise His reign over every aspect of our lives.

I have shared different stages in my own journey. I reflect on times of completion and fulfilment: from graduations to ordination, from building Kingdom churches and projects to marriage and seeing our children marry and have families of their own. These involved struggles and overcoming, endings and beginnings. My retirement after forty years of ministry was a time of culmination and conclusion, yet it is also a time of looking forward to a new beginning. I look back with a sense of gratitude at the abundance of opportunities that I have been given and enjoyed. All of these specific events are steps along the way as I head toward that event we all will face, our final day on this earth before joining the saints in heaven. There we will stand before the Lord and find out how we fulfilled His call and commission. It is my and all our hope, I'm sure, to hear His voice saying, "Well done, my good and faithful servant." At whatever stage of life we find ourselves, today is the day we can still start right in order to complete the race and finish well.

We look up and look forward towards the finishing line, to the return of our Lord and the consummation of His kingdom.

The Spirit and the bride say, Come!...
Amen. Come, Lord Jesus!
(Revelation 22:17, 20)

Questions

If Jesus is King and rules with authority, what areas of your life need to come under His rulership?

As disciples who reigns with Him, how can we exercise that authority?

As we pray and walk with Jesus, how do we see Him? Which of the descriptions of the Ascended Lord in John's vision speak to you the most?

God offers himself to us as Almighty God, Wonderful Counselor, Everlasting Father, Prince of Peace. How have you been able to know Him in all these ways? What do you most need from Him at the moment?

Let's pray! Lord Jesus Christ we ask you to be:

The Prince of peace who breathes the Holy Spirit of peace into our life situations.

The King who reigns within our hearts, our relationships, our homes, our work, our churches, our cities, our nations.

The Saviour who redeems that which seems lost and beyond hope.

The Judge who convicts and corrects, cleanses and transforms, refines and purifies.

The Light who reveals, directs, warms, and opens up all possibilities so that we might experience life in all its fullness.

The Alpha and the Omega who offers us a new start every day and sustains us through to the end.

In the midst of Your Church in all the fullness of the Holy Spirit.

CHECK OUT THESE OTHER BOOKS BY ROD!

King of Hearts

Come Let Us Build